Guadalupe
A River of Light

THE STORY OF OUR LADY OF GUADALUPE FROM THE FIRST
CENTURY TO OUR DAYS

Carlos Caso-Rosendi

Edited by Patricia Stafford

3/2023

Alayna,

May Mother Mary
guide you all
through your life
closer to Jesus.

Love,
     Grandma & Grandpa Mayer

ISBN: 9 7819 7706 0181
Copyright © 2017 Carlos Caso-Rosendi
This book is also available in Spanish and Portuguese.
All rights reserved.
FIRST LIGHT PRESS

In Memoriam
GIORGIO SERNANI
1940-2014

Acknowledgements

The author would like to express his special gratitude to all those who contributed with their prayers, work, and financial help to complete and publish this book.

Ad majorem Dei gloriam

Published by First Light Press
Front Royal, Virginia, United States of America
This book is also available in Spanish and Portuguese

Obsequium Religiosum

The author of this book believes and assents with absolute submission of mind and will to the authentic Magisterium of the Roman Catholic Church, and reverently recognizes the judgments of the Roman Pontiff, accepting them sincerely in toto. The author humbly requests a quick fraternal correction if any unintentional error conflicting with Catholic doctrine is found in this book.

Unless indicated otherwise, the biblical texts cited have been translated by the author, taking as reference various translations of the Latin Vulgate that are commonly used.

CONTENTS

THE REVELATION TO SAINT JOHN 22:1-7

Then the angel showed me the River of the Water of Life, bright as crystal, flowing from the throne of God and of the Lamb through the middle of the street of the city. On either side of the river is the tree of life with its twelve kinds of fruit, producing its fruit each month; and the leaves of the tree are for the healing of the nations. Nothing impure will be found there anymore. The throne of God and of the Lamb will be in it, and His servants will worship him; they will see His face, and His Name will be on their foreheads. And there will be no more night; they need no light of lamp or sun, for the Lord God will be their light, and they will reign for ever and ever. And he said to me: "These words are trustworthy and true, for the Lord, the God of the spirits of the prophets, has sent his angel to show his servants what must soon take place. See, I am coming soon! Blessed is the one who keeps the words of the prophecy of this book."

UNLESS THERE IS SUPERNATURAL HELP

It was December 12, 1531. On the day of the solstice of winter for the northern hemisphere when the Julian Calendar was still in use, a humble man named Juan Diego Cuauhtlatoatzin, of the Chichimeca tribe was swiftly moving towards Mexico with a mission. He was a native Mexican, a witness to the fall of the Aztec Empire and the Spanish conquest. He was also a convert to the faith of the conquerors patiently preached to him by the priests sent from Spain by King Charles V.

In a day like today, the Speaking Eagle was on his way to see Don Juan Zumárraga, the Catholic Bishop sent by the king with extraordinary temporal powers. Mexico was a tinderbox ready to ignite in a civil war. Don Juan Zumárraga was struggling to see how he could preserve his faithful from the opposing parties: the natives that refused to convert to the faith, and the avaricious party of Spaniards who wanted to keep the natives ignorant and pagan, with the intention of exploiting them at will.

Poor Don Zumárraga had spent the previous night praying and asking God for help. The task he had been assigned was overwhelming, impossible. Recently he had sent a sad but sincere assessment of the situation in a secret message to King Charles: "Unless there is supernatural help, the country is lost." He prayed on his knees until late, begging for God's help. He was at the end of his wits, running out of time as the social forces at play prepared for a violent clash. About the time the Bishop finished his prayers and went to sleep, the Speaking Eagle was beginning his descent from Tepeyac Hill.

The Eagle descends on the lake

Juan Diego carried a message from Heaven: fresh, fragrant Castilian roses wrapped in his tilma. He was not walking but running with that steady indian trot that devours mile after mile. He had learned the secret coordination of moving and breathing from his ancestors who had crossed the high plains of Mexico since times immemorial. The morning star was rising over the city still asleep when he saw the bridges and the lake in the distance, reflecting the moon on the quiet waters. He went through the gates with the first light of day and marched to the Bishop's residence through the silent streets.

There he waited patiently several hours until late morning. The guards and the Bishop's attendants abused poor Juan by letting him wait in the cold for hours while Don Zumárraga went through his daily routine. After the morning Mass ended, the Bishop was approached by a native family – we know all these details by deduction, after modern technology studied the reflections on Our Lady's eyes. The young couple came to greet him after presenting their newborn for baptism. Their friends were there, the godfather and godmother of the baby, their other child, and a man who played music. Music was not meant merely to entertain. Mexicans always associate music with all kinds of events: arrivals, departures, birthdays, funerals, marriages. The natives understood that music was a connection with the world beyond, a sound with the mysterious power to lift or soothe the soul. Remember that the first contact of Juan Diego with Our Lady was through the song of birds. Our Lady of Guadalupe was thus introducing herself in a very Mexican way, with music.

The party of thirteen people were gathering behind the heavy entrance doors. Right outside, still in waiting after five or six hours of patiently enduring the cold temperature, was our man Juan Diego. He had no intention to quit. He was perfectly quiet, like the eagle guarding the nest endures the cold wind while perched on a high peak. Juan Diego's eyes were fixed on the eternal, much like the eagle's eyes scanning the deep valley from the inaccesible mountain heights.

Two of the servants decided to question Juan Diego. They did not want that low macehualtin there. They had not informed the Bishop that a man was waiting for him outside in the cold. They approached Juan Diego and demanded to see what he was carrying. As he refused they tried to grab the edge of his cloak. Juan Diego could see that he could not keep his precious cargo from the two annoying men, so he decided to allow them to take a peek at the flowers. Of course the two men were amazed that such precious flowers could be in bloom during winter. They tried to grab one rose but every time they tried, it disappeared into the fabric and they could not hold it.

After three tries they panicked. Was this man a sorcerer? He could be the devil himself, or a demon! Scared out of their minds they busted into the chamber where the Bishop was receiving a family ... One of them dragged Juan Diego before the Bishop. Everything happened so fast that Juan Diego did not have a chance to take off his hat. There he was before all those important people, still with his hat on, like a crowned king holding court. Our Lady had promised him: "I will grant you honor and glory" and this was the moment for that. Juan Diego was entering history. The Speaking Eagle had landed just like the old Mexican Eagle of the Aztec legend had touched down on the nopal. There he was in the city – located in the middle of the lake – standing before the most powerful man in Mexico, Bishop Zumárraga, the official envoy of King Charles V of Spain, the Ruler of the Holy Roman Empire.

Juan Diego entered the room and knelt before the Prelate telling him once again the marvels that he had seen: "Dear Bishop, I have done what you asked me to do. I told the Lady from Heaven, my Lady, my Heavenly beloved, Holy Mary, the Mother of God, that you have asked her for a sign so you could believe my message: that a little house is built in the place where she asked it to be erected. I also told her that I have promised you to come back with a sign, a proof of her will, just as you asked. She listened to your insistence, to your words, and she was pleased to receive your request for a sign so that her precious will might be accomplished. Early today when it was still dark she told me to come here to see you. I reminded her that she had promised to give me a sign that I could bring to you.

She immediately fulfilled her word. She sent me to the hilltop where I had seen her before, to cut various kinds of roses and once I cut them I presented a bunch to her. She took them in her holy hands and arranged them in the fold of my ayate so that I could bring them and give them to you in person. I knew very well that the top of the Tepeyac was not a place to find flowers in bloom since that is a place where nothing ever grows except thorny bushes, prickly pears, and mesquites in the midst of crags and rocks; I did not hesitate to go. When I climbed to the top of the hill I found a Paradise. There were all kinds of beautiful flowers, the finest flowers, covered with dewdrops, blooming splendidly, so I proceeded to cut a bunch. She instructed me to give you these flowers on her behalf so her precious will might be accomplished once you see the proof you have asked for. Now, believe the truth of my words. Here you have them, please accept them."

Then Juan Diego opened the fold of his tilma where the flowers were placed. As he allowed the beautiful flowers to cascade to the ground they were changed into a sign: the beloved image of the Perfect Virgin Holy Mary, Mother of God, suddenly appeared in the same figure that we now behold in her precious little house, her holy little place in Tepeyac that is called Guadalupe. And when the Bishop and all who were there saw her, they fell to their knees and marveled greatly at her. (Taken from chapter 4, The Conversion of Mexico quoting the Nican Mopohua by Antonio Valeriano.)

Our Lady had promised him: "I will give you honor and glory" and there was Juan Diego, standing in the middle of a circle of people, his betters kneeling before him, honoring him like a king. The image of Our Lady had materialized on Juan's tilma in an awesome display of God's power.

Think of the scene: the family represents the people of Mexico, the Spanish men represent the race that came from across the sea, Don Zumárraga represents the Pope and the Holy Roman Emperor... but Juan Diego, called by Our Lady as "Juan Diegotzin, my little one" represents the Mother of the King of Kings. God Himself had sent his ambassador to

Mexico, the Speaking Eagle Cuauhtlatoatzin: "[God] says, 'It is too small a thing that You should be My Servant to raise up the tribes of Jacob and to restore the preserved ones of Israel; I will also make you a light of the nations so that my salvation may reach to the ends of the earth.'" – Isaiah 49:6.

He has not dealt thus with any other nation

The Law given to Israel carries in itself the proof of its divine origin. The Gospel of Jesus Christ given to his Church is a marvel of obvious supernatural origin. The image of Our Lady of Guadalupe is also a miraculous communication, and a sign. The time, the people involved, the manner in which all happened, everything around the events of 1531 in Mexico are nothing but a huge parable set up by the unfathomable power of God to teach us something akin to the Law and the Gospel. This message of salvation is a call to action. The Americas were a world much like our own global civilization: completely controlled by the spiritual forces of evil. Through a miracle of communication that surpasses any of the modern technological achievements of man, Our Lady of Guadalupe gave birth to a new Christian nation using that impossible canvas, the tilma. Imprinted on that humble cloak there was a message for Mexico and the world that still resonates even in our age.

Today, the Americas are reverting to the darkness of error and paganism. The old abominable practices are returning like weeds growing on a tilled field. Even the Church is infected with the practices of the ancient American religions: ritual homosexuality, widespread fornication, human sacrifice in the form of abortion, and worse. This is the time to pray like Don Juan Zumárraga did on the eve of December 12, 1531: "Unless there is supernatural help, the country is lost."

On your day, dear Mother we pray. Please obtain for us the grace of purifying and saving our world and our Church. Teach us to follow the example of your favorite son, St Juan Diego Cuauhtlatoatzin and help us speak your pure word of salvation to this age lost in darkness.

"God comes … before him goes pestilence, and the plague follows in his steps. He pauses to survey the earth; his look makes the nations tremble. The eternal mountains are shattered, the age-old hills bow low along his ancient ways … in wrath you bestride the earth; in fury, you trample the nations. You come forth to save your people, to save your anointed one. You crush the heads of the wicked, you lay bare their bases at the neck. You pierce with your shafts the heads of their princes whose boast would be of devouring the wretched in their lair. You tread the sea with your steeds amid the churning of the deep waters …"

PREFACE

The idea for this book came to me in the wee hours of the morning of April 2, 2017, after reading about the origins of the Royal Monastery of Santa Maria de Guadalupe, which is located in the town of the same name in Extremadura, Spain. The imposing building has humble origins harking back to the days of King Alfonso XI of Castile who was born on August 13, 1311 and died on March 26, 1350. He was called "El Justiciero" (*Sp.* avenger, dispenser of justice) and held the crowns of the Christian kingdoms of Castile, Leon, and Galicia.[1] His father was Ferdinand IV of Castile. He married Princess Mary, daughter of Alfonso IV of Portugal, known as "El Bravo" (*Sp.* fierce, brave). During the reign of Alfonso XI, the Virgin Mary appeared to a peasant called Gil Cordero and revealed to him the location of certain relics buried in a cave near the Guadalupe River. Among those relics, there was a carved image of the Virgin and Child, known today as Our Lady of Guadalupe. King Alfonso XI and his peer of Portugal, Alfonso IV invoked the help of Mary, Mother of God before the Battle of Rio Salado where the combined Christian armies of Spain and Portugal were facing vastly superior Muslim forces. After the battle, Alfonso of Castile credited the resounding Christian victory to the intercession of the Madonna. In gratefulness, he declared the church at Guadalupe a royal sanctuary, rebuilding the modest original structure into a magnificent Romanic church that survives until today.

As I was reading the story of Gil Cordero, I was reminded of St Juan Diego Cuauhtlatoatzin, the Mexican visionary of Tepeyac to whom the Virgin Mary appeared in 1531, also as Our Lady of Guadalupe. Soon I noticed some parallelism between the two stories. Both Gil and Juan Diego were humble men, both exemplary Christians and family men. Gil Cordero returned home to find his child dead but the child resurrected miraculously. Juan Diego's uncle Juan Bernardino was cured of a life-threatening illness in a similar way. Most importantly, Gil and Juan Diego were living in times of profound

---

[1] Alfonso XI, "El Onceno" (*Sp.* The Eleventh) was a descendant of Alfonso X "El Sabio" (*Sp.* The Wise.) Alfonso XI was also the third great grandfather of Queen Isabella of Castile, "La Católica", (*Sp.* The Catholic).

religious and political change. The Spanish man saw the expulsion of the last Muslim Moors and the consolidation of Spain under a Christian monarchy; his Mexican counterpart witnessed the political and religious end of the Aztec Empire and the birth of Mexico as a Christian nation.

Those would be nothing but a chance collection of similarities were it not for the fact that the Virgin Mary introduced herself to Juan Diego Cuauhtlatoatzin as "Our Lady of Guadalupe"—the name Guadalupe inevitably connects the two stories supernaturally. Later, I took a step back and considered the origin of the Spanish image and its Mexican counterpart and began to suspect that both images could be the work of the same author. Unfortunately, that will remain a mere suspicion since I am not able to interview St Luke. According to well-documented tradition, St Luke carved the image now in Extremadura at some point during the first century. The image was deposited along with him in his burial place in Thebes, Greece and was later taken to Constantinople with his relics.

That utterly fantastic possibility led me to meditate about the long trail traced by that image through history from the times of the Byzantine Empire, to the times of Emperor Moctezuma, and then to our own days. That humble image somehow was present at the fall of three great dominions: the Roman Empire, Moorish Spain, and the Aztec Empire. In time, I had a chance to read about how scientists in the 20th century, by using the latest scanning technology, discovered thirteen people "photographed" in the eyes of the image depicted in Juan Diego's tilma. That extraordinary discovery made me aware that the image not only contained a message for the Mexican people of the 16th century but also had a word for the future generations of mankind. The author of the image of Our Lady of Guadalupe patiently waited four centuries until men could work with more advanced technology, in order to read that hidden message in the Virgin's eyes.

Often I have to endure some well-intentioned Protestant friend reading from Psalm 115:4-6 "Their idols are silver and gold, the work of man's hands. They have mouths, but they cannot speak; they have eyes, but they cannot see; they have ears, but they cannot hear; they have noses, but they cannot smell." That is, of course, a misguided judgment of the use of images in Catholic worship. The image on Juan Diego's tilma has been found to contain in its eyes a scene perfectly defined. No one has been able to determine how it was painted. Perhaps the best definition was given by those who saw it appear miraculously on the modest cloth "as if it was painted by angels" because it is definitely not the product of human hands.

I gradually came to understand that both Our Lady of Guadalupe in Spain and Our Lady of Guadalupe in Mexico are part of a majestic parable presented to us across centuries of Christian history. I tried in vain to condense the many aspects of that divine parable in a few words. The many facets presented to us are so deep in meaning, so rich in wonderful lessons that they can only come from God Almighty.

To unveil the grand parable, we have to weave our way through history going back and forth in time to understand important details. The reader will forgive me for not following a strict chronological order. More than looking at a succession of events in time, we will be looking through the many branches of an ancient tree. Intertwined among those branches there is a lesson that we must contemplate before we can understand it completely.

The center of the grand parable is Blessed Mary. God the creator of Mary of Nazareth has decided to teach us the ways of justice and peace through her. God is light (1 John 1:5) and He presents to us His Mother fully illuminated, dressed as it were, in a wave of light. In the 1940s, Sister Maria Lucia de Jesus Rosa Santos,[2] at that time the last surviving visionary of Fatima, used these words to describe the mantle of Our Lady to Fr. Thomas McGlynn: "The mantle was a wave of light" and regarding the mantle and tunic: "There were two waves of light, one on top of the other." That simple but powerful observation by Sister Lucia call to mind these verses of the Apocalypse of St John: "And a great portent appeared in heaven, a woman clothed with the sun, with the moon under her feet, and on her head a crown of twelve stars; she was with child and she cried out in her pangs of birth, in anguish for delivery." These verses in Revelation 12:1-3 perfectly reveal both a Mother of Light and a Mother of Sorrows.

We were taught that the woman of Revelation 12 is Israel that later becomes the Christian Church continually giving birth to the faithful through the ages. I believe the scene may also represent Our Blessed Mother, the Mother of the Savior of Israel and the indisputable Mother of all faithful Christians. After all, she was the only perfect daughter of Israel, the sacred vessel that contained in herself the life of Christ. Therefore, she was the first Church, the first evangelizer, and the first disciple of her Son. Some believe that whoever saves a man's life saves all the generations coming from that man. How could the Mother of the Messiah—Savior of Israel and the human race—not be the Mother of all those whom He saved by giving them eternal life? Who else is clothed with the Sun, surrounded by the light of God, as she who was born full of grace?[3]

---

[2] The name Maria Lucia de Jesus Rosa Santos strangely calls to mind many Marian elements of Guadalupe: Mary, light (*Lat.* Lucia, "born at dawn" or "luminous"), Jesus, rose, and saints. Maria Lucia is also the name of Juan Diego's wife.

[3] Luke 1: 28.

Before going into the lessons in this marvelous parable painted by God on the canvas of space and time, please consider the words of Jesus in the Gospel of John: God shows us history as the development of His purpose: to give life to mankind. To give us life, God gave us a Mother first.[4]

---

[4] John 10:10.

1

A GOLDEN THREAD

This thread through history begins with the Immaculate Conception and continues through the great Apostolic Age and beyond. The story was hidden until St Juan Diego Cuauhtlatoatzin (1474-1548), a humble Chichimeca Indian, met the Blessed Virgin Mary on Tepeyac Hill, almost five centuries ago. The tilma of St Juan Diego bearing the miraculous image appears in history in what is now Mexico, the morning of December 12, 1531, almost forty years after Columbus set foot in the American continent and about ten years after the conquest of Mexico by Hernan Cortez.[5] The man whose destiny was to be the conqueror of Mexico was born in Spain, most precisely in Medellin, in a city located in the province of Badajoz in the region of Extremadura. About sixty miles northeast from his birthplace lay the town of Guadalupe in the province of Caceres. There are various possible etymologies for the name of Guadalupe. One of the most logical is derived from the original Roman name *Flumen Lux Speculum*—meaning "a river reflecting light"—a name that the Mozarab settlers may have mispronounced and finally passed into Spanish as *Rio Guadalupejo*. Some believe the first two syllables are the remnant of the Arabic word for river: *wad*.[6]

---

[5] His complete name was: Hernán Cortés de Monroy y Pizarro Altamirano

[6] The origin of the word is uncertain. Some etymologists affirm that "Guadalupe" is composed of "wad" (river), "al" (article) and "lub" (black stone) because the river carried black stones. Others suggest the alternative "Wad al lubben" (hidden river) since the Guadalupe River runs through deep gorges that hid its presence. In the author's opinion, the Arabic name most likely sounded somewhat close to the word "Guadalupe." The modern name possibly evolved from 15th century Castilian luspejo, or aguada del espejo, meaning literally "watering hole [through, a place where animals drink] of the mirror" by apocopation to Guadalupejo, a local name that is still in use. In the name "Guadalupe" the final particle "ejo" is eliminated possibly because that particle carries sometimes a derogatory connotation. *See Historia de Guadalupe by Fray Gabriel Talavera. Toledo 1597,*

In this first chapter, we are going very summarily through thousands of years of history covering some relevant events from the early days of Christianity to the end of the Middle Ages in Spain, and then a brief chronicle of the New World before the arrival of the first Europeans. It is only a bird's eye view but I promise you that going through all that history is going to pay off wonderfully because every stage of the story is going to be opened in the subsequent chapters. In the end, I hope you will see very clearly the hand of God working a grand parable that will unfold as something so spectacular that only the Almighty could have done it. In the center of that grand parable is humble Mary of Nazareth, the greatest woman that will ever live.

Saint Luke the Artist

The town of Guadalupe is home to one of the great treasures of Christianity, an image of the Virgin Mary holding the Child that according to ancient Christian traditions was carved by St Luke, the author of the Gospel that bears his name. St Luke's original name may have been Lucanus;[7] we know he was born in Antioch of Syria and it is likely that he studied medicine in Tarsus. In Colossians 4:14, St Paul calls him "the beloved physician." Through Nicaphorus Callistus (14th century), and the *Menology of Basil II* (10th century) we know he was also a painter.

The Catholic Encyclopedia declares: "A picture of the Virgin in Santa Maria Maggiore, Rome, is ascribed to him and can be traced to A.D. 847. It is probably a copy of that mentioned by Theodore Lector, in the sixth century. This writer states that the Empress Eudoxia found a picture of the Mother of God at Jerusalem, which she sent to Constantinople (see "Acta SS." of 18 October). As Plummer observes, it is certain that St Luke was an artist, at least to the extent that his graphic descriptions of the Annunciation, Visitation, Nativity, Shepherds, Presentation, the Good Shepherd, etc., have become the inspiring and favorite themes of Christian painters."[8]

From all the information we have about St Luke, we can safely deduct that he was Greek, a convert to Judaism who later accepted Christianity. He was also a dedicated evangelist who traveled with St Paul and St Mark.[9] The brief introduction found in Luke 1:1-4 shows that he was dedicated to accurately preserving the truth of the Gospel, researching the facts from very early witnesses.

"Many have undertaken to draw up an account of the things that have

---

fol. 9-11 and *El Origen del nombre de Guadalupe* by Arturo Alvares. *Historia de Nuestra Señora de Guadalupe y Fray Francisco de San José* by Germán Rubio; and *Historia Universal de la Primitiva y Milagrosa Imagen de Nuestra Señora de Guadalupe*, Madrid, 1763.

[7] The meaning of the name Lucanus is "circled, surrounded by light".

[8] The Gospel of St Luke, as quoted online in newadvent.com.

[9] See Acts 16:8; 2 Timothy 4:7-11; Colossians 4:14, and Philemon 24.

been fulfilled among us, just as they were handed down to us by those who from the first were eyewitnesses and servants of the Word. With this in mind, since I myself have carefully investigated everything from the beginning, I too decided to write an orderly account for you, most excellent Theophilus, so that you may know the certainty of the things you have been taught."[10]

The Gospel According to St Luke is often called "the Gospel of Mary" and it is certain that Luke had the opportunity to know and interview Mary of Nazareth while she was living in Ephesus.

The early Christian traditions in Europe talk of many paintings and sculptures of Our Lady attributed to St Luke. The amazing story of Our Lady of Guadalupe begins with an image that was buried with him when he died. In *De Viris Illustribus*[11] St Jerome reports "his bones and relics are buried in Constantinople, transferred there along with those of the Apostle Andrew."[12]

St Luke died in Thebes in the Bœotia region of ancient Greece at the age of seventy-four.[13] A statuette representing the Virgin and Child—carved by Luke himself—was buried with him.

To Constantinople and Rome

The coffin containing the remains of St Luke was transferred to Constantinople by order of the Roman Emperor Flavius Julius Constantius Augustus in A.D. 357. The Italian historian Flavio Ciucani—author of *Il Segreto negli Occhi di Maria. Da Nazareth a Guadalupe*—affirms: "With a great procession, the coffin containing the remains of St Luke went into the Church escorted by all the imperial court. Leading them was Macedonius, the Bishop of Constantinople. He held the statuette above his head as the procession continued along the central nave."[14]

Mauritius (A.D. 539-590), Emperor of the Eastern Roman Empire, gave the image to future Pope Gregory the Great in A.D. 582. At that time, Gregory was the Papal Ambassador to the imperial court in Constantinople.

---

[10] Luke 1:1-4.

[11] *De Viris Illustribus*, (On Illustrious Famous Men) by St Jerome, Scriptura Press, New York City, 2015.

[12] "Sepultus est Constantinopoli, ad quam urbem vigesimo Constantii anno, ossa ejus cum reliquiis Andreæ Apostoli translata sunt." *De Viris Illustribus* 3, 7.

[13] "After St Paul's martyrdom practically all that is known about him is contained in the ancient Prefatio vel Argumentum Lucæ, dating back to Julius Africanus, who was born circa A.D. 165. This states that he was unmarried, that he wrote the Gospel, in Achaia, and that he died at the age of seventy-four in Bithynia (probably a copyist's error for Bœotia), filled with the Holy Ghost." Catholic Encyclopedia; The Gospel of St Luke, as quoted online in newadvent.com.

[14] *Il Segreto negli Occhi di Maria – Da Nazareth a Guadalupe*, (The Secret in Mary's Eyes—from Nazareth to Guadalupe) by Flavio Ciucani, Edizione Mediterranee, Roma, 2013. Quotation translated by the author.

When Gregory returned to Rome in 582, the statuette went with him. About that time, Rome suffered a terrible epidemic that caused the death of many, among them Pope Pelagius II. Gregory was elected to succeed him. This is the same Gregory who is now known as St Gregory the Great. He ordered the people to recite the litanies and took the miraculous image of Our Lady in procession. This was no other than the image of Our Lady that Pope Gregory had kept in his private oratory until that day. While the procession was crossing Rome, the people heard a choir of angels singing praises to the Virgin Mary, saying:

"Queen of Heaven, rejoice, for He whom you did merit to bear, has risen, as he said."

After the singing, one angel appeared over the building now known as Castel Sant'Angelo, wiping the blood off his sword.[15] After that, the plague ceased and St Gregory gratefully grew in his devotion to Our Lady's image.[16]

A few years later, Gregory sent several relics to the Archbishop of Seville, St Leander who had worked tirelessly to eradicate the Arian heresy. Among those relics was St Luke's statuette of the Virgin and Child.

A storm endangered the ship while the statuette was traveling by sea from Rome to Seville. At that point, a priest took the image onto the ship's deck and begged piously to Our Lady to end the tempest. His prayer was immediately answered and so they could safely reach Seville. St Leander, Bishop of Seville and a friend of Pope Gregory received the image in person. The image was later enthroned in the Cathedral of Seville where it was fervently venerated by the local Christians.

In A.D. 711, Seville came under attack by Muslim invaders. Some of the local Christians, carrying the precious relic, escaped the city towards the north of Spain, following the Via Lusitana. As they approached the region now known as Extremadura, they buried the image in a mountainous area near a stream we know today as the Guadalupe River. Along with the image, there was documentation identifying the statue's origin and other relics as well. The image was to remain buried there six centuries.

Buried and Found Again

In the summer of 1329 when the Christian reconquest of Spain was almost completed, and King Alfonso XI reigned in Castile, a Christian settler named Gil Cordero was shepherding his cattle in the area of the Guadalupe River. When Gil realized that one of his cows was missing, he went in search of the animal. After three days, he found it dead near the river. Disappointed by the loss, he decided to skin the animal to save the hide. As he unsheathed his

---

[15] Please see 2 Samuel 24:11-25 where there is a similar angelic intervention.
[16] *The Spanish History of Our Lady of Guadalupe Prior to the 16th Century Apparitions in Mexico*, by Sister Gabriel, OP, 1900.

knife, the animal came back to life before his very eyes. Instantly, the figure of a woman bathed in light appeared floating above him. The woman then spoke saying:

"Do not be afraid. I am the Mother of God the Savior of the human race. Take your cow and return it to the corral with the others and then go back home. Tell the priests what you have seen. Tell them also that you are sent to them on my behalf. They must come to this place where you are now and dig where the dead cow was; under these stones, you will find an image of mine. When they unearth it tell them not to take it nor move it away. They must erect a chapel for it. In time, a great church, a noble house, and a great nation will grow around this place."[17]

Obediently, Gil Cordero walked to Caceres and related to the authorities what he had seen but no one believed him. When he arrived home perturbed by all the things he had experienced, he found his wife in the company of some neighbors and religious, crying because their son had just died. The poor man looking at the lifeless body of his son remembered how the Virgin Mary had resurrected his cow. Without further reflection he knelt, and trusting wholeheartedly in Our Lady with sincere devotion he begged:

"My Lady, you know the message that I am bringing on your behalf, I believe it to be true that you brought this about: that my son is dead because in this way you will show how marvelous you are in bringing him back to life so that this message of yours that I was sent to deliver will be believed quickly. If that is so, my Lady, I beg you to resurrect him. Here and from now on I offer him to you, to be your perpetual servant in the place where you gave me the grace of appearing before me."

His sincere prayer seemed to go unanswered. The clergy prayed, and finally, the body of his son was taken to the cemetery. On the way there, the child sat erect in the coffin and begged his father to take him to the Mountain of Guadalupe so that he might give thanks to the Blessed Virgin for restoring his life. The miracle happened in the presence of many witnesses, confirming to all that Gil Cordero was telling the truth about the apparition of Our Lady. Gil addressed the crowd with words of faith:

"My lords and friends, please know that this had to happen so you can put faith in the message that I bring. Our Lady has given us the grace to perform this great marvel since due to our sin often we doubt those things we cannot contemplate with our own senses."

The story of that prodigy traveled quickly and reached those who had not

---

[17] The prophecy of Our Lady came to pass. The Church in Spain was entering its golden age, producing many saints and a rich spirituality; the scattered kingdoms of former Roman Hispania became Spain, a bastion of Christianity that took the faith across the globe; and finally Spain itself became a crucible where her many races forged the Spanish national identity into one, great, and free nation.

believed at first. The authorities were now convinced that something supernatural had occurred. They followed Gil to the place by the river and unearthed a marble box containing the image of Our Lady, along with other relics, and some documents relating the origin and history of the statuette, from the time when it was carved by St Luke, until the time when it was buried by the men of Seville.

In the box, they found the wooden image of Our Lady, along with documents stating the date of its concealment, more than six hundred years before. They also found an ancient bell, the relics of the siblings of St Leander and St Isidore: St Fulgentius and St Florentine.[18] The clergy and people thought of returning to town with the image, but Gil Cordero insisted that they could not disobey the instructions of the Virgin Mary. Everyone agreed and they built a temporary chapel to house the image. Pilgrims who visit the monastery today can still see the rough stone altar upon which the statue rested. Gil Cordero and his family remained near the humble sanctuary that we now know as the Shrine of Our Lady of Guadalupe.

The prophecy of Our Lady was fulfilled. The kings of Spain and Portugal and their nobility traveled in pilgrimage often to that sacred place. Spain grew strong around it, growing from a loose confederation of Christian fiefdoms into a great Christian country under one crown. Spain became a great empire spreading the Gospel of Jesus Christ all over the world. The Spanish Church produced some of the great saints: St Teresa of Avila, St John of the Cross, St Ignatius Loyola, St Dominic of Guzman, St Joseph of Calasanz, St Angela of the Cross, St Vincent Ferrer, St Francis Xavier, and so many others, too long a list to complete here.

Guadalupe and the Kings of Spain

In time, King Alfonso XI visited the humble chapel and ordered it to be enlarged so that it would become a temple worthy of the precious relics there contained. Gradually a town began to grow around the sanctuary. Since those days, the fame of Guadalupe extended far outside Spain. Since the foundation of the village of Guadalupe, it became a tradition for the Kings of Castile to visit the place. The Habsburgs did not break that pious royal custom that was later interrupted to be started again by King Alfonso XIII. King Enrique IV

---

[18] When the Visigoths ruled Spain, there lived a nobleman called Severianus, son of King Theodoric Amalus, Ostrogoth and King of Italy who ruled Spain on behalf of his young grandson Amalric. Severianus was raised by his mother receiving from her the rudiments of the Catholic faith. Severianus, Duke of Carthage (Murcia, Spain) married Theodora who was also of noble lineage. They had five children: St Leander, St Fulgentius, and St Florentine, St Isidore, and St Theodosia—according to historian Eduardo Cabañete Navarro—she married Liuvigild and was the mother of King St Hermenegild (a martyr) and King Recaredo.

of Castile and his mother Queen Maria of Aragon are buried in the monastery.

From the time of its foundation, the Mother of God did not cease to bless the sanctuary of Guadalupe with many graces.[19] Many great men and women of Spain, including the royal families, found rest and encouragement there to continue the expansion of the Empire. It would be impossible to list all of the noble pilgrims that visited the place but we can list a few. When his wise minister Don Alvaro de Luna died, King Juan II took one of the monks in the monastery as his counselor. Maria de Aragon and Enrique IV had a monk from Guadalupe as their confessor, Father Cabañuelas who had experienced one of the most spectacular Eucharistic miracles of that age.

The lives of Queen Isabella of Castile and King Ferdinand of Aragon are very connected with Guadalupe. She visited the monastery many times, always seeking St Mary's protection and guidance. Isabella gave orders that her royal testament be kept there forever. By the intercession of the Virgin Mary, King Ferdinand's life was miraculously spared after an assassination attempt. Many years after, he died there in Guadalupe.

The whole of Spain was integrated politically as a nation during the reign of Ferdinand and Isabella. Religious unity was also completed after the fall of Granada, and the conquest was followed by the first evangelization of the Americas.

Through the faithful prayers of the monks in the monastery, Isabella devotedly trusted to Our Blessed Mother the final military campaign against the Moors. Once the city was conquered, she sent a grateful letter to the monks of Guadalupe. Later both King and Queen visited the sanctuary on June 9 of 1492 to give thanks to God for the victory.

On June 20 of 1488, royal letters were signed giving Juan de Peñalosa the authority to commission three vessels and their crews under Christopher Columbus to find a western passage to India. Queen Isabella of Castile and Ferdinand of Aragon received Columbus there. After the final great battle of the Reconquest—when the last of the Muslim enclaves was recovered—the royal couple came to Guadalupe to rest and venerate the image; at various times Christopher Columbus did the same.

In 1492 as the last of the Moors were being expelled from Spain, Columbus' expedition departed from the port of Palos in Andalusia. Our Lady of Guadalupe saved the mission when the small fleet had to face a very fierce storm in the Azores. In the midst of that terrible tempest, the Admiral and

---

[19] The mission of Our Lady of Guadalupe appeared to be one of liberation and protection. The walls of the sanctuary still show the chains of many prisoners captured by the Moors who were liberated by the efforts of various religious orders. There are reports of prisoners miraculously translated from Africa directly to that Church. The Franciscans keep a record of miraculous events that is several volumes long.

crew entrusted their salvation to her. Making solemn vows, they drew lots to determine who would make a special pilgrimage to her sanctuary. The sacred obligation fell on Columbus himself who fulfilled the promise promptly when they arrived safely in Spain. For that reason, Columbus gave the name Guadalupe to the first island they discovered.

On July 29, 1496, Columbus symbolically consecrated all the spiritual first fruits of the New World by bringing two American natives to the sanctuary. Both were baptized in front of the image carved by St Luke fourteen centuries earlier.

Christopher Columbus

The Americas remained hidden from the rest of the world up until the arrival of Columbus and the first Spanish explorers.

There were previous encounters between Europe and America but contacts between Native Americans and foreign people were very rare or infrequent until that morning of October 12, 1492, when Admiral Columbus set foot for the first time on what he called Hispaniola Island.

We must make a pause in our story to take a look at this man, Christopher Columbus, whose historical figure becomes more and more important as years go by. Cristóforo Colombo—that was his original name—was a native of Genoa. That city in northern Italy had been for many centuries home to famous bankers, traders, shipbuilders, and sailors.

Some historians claim that Columbus was a member of a devout Jewish family converted to Christianity. His name seems to confirm that. In those days, converts from Judaism used to take some particular names (from trees, birds, or their specific trade) to indicate where they were coming from and, therefore, to be able to recognize each other after their conversion.

"Colombo" means "dove" in many Italian dialects – that is also the name of the Prophet Jonah[20]—while Christopher means "the Christ-bearer." That is also St Christopher's name, a very popular saint with Genoese sailors and tradesmen.

The Offerus Connection

It is widely claimed that the saints we select to bless our baptism and confirmation imprint some of their virtues on our souls. This seems to be especially true regarding Christopher Columbus. In those days, St Christopher was the patron saint of travelers.

As the legend goes, St Christopher was a very strong man from Canaan who was looking to serve the greatest of all masters. Having learned that Christ was the greatest of them all, Offerus—as he was called before

---

[20] The Hebrew name יוֹנָה (Yonah) means "dove"—Jonah was the prophet sent by God to preach in Nineveh. He fled from his divine appointment by boat but he was caught in a storm. The prophet was thrown overboard and was swallowed by a big fish. Three days later he emerged alive, repentant and ready to fulfill his mission, which resulted in the conversion of Nineveh.

becoming a Christian—came upon a holy man, and asked him where he could find Christ. The holy man taught him to use his strength to perform works of mercy since the best way to serve Christ is to serve others. He instructed Offerus to go and find out some broad, deep river, with a swift current that men could not cross. Offerus found a suitable river and dedicated his strength to help those who struggled to cross, carrying on his broad shoulders the weak and the small. Offerus built a hut on the bank of that river and dwelled there. Whenever someone tried to cross the stream, Offerus helped him. The legend tells us that one night, as he was resting, he heard the voice of a child, saying: "Offerus, will you help me cross?" He went to the bank of the river, but he could not find anyone. Three times he heard the mysterious call and searched until he came upon a little child, who begged him: "Offerus carry me over!" He lifted the child and began to cross the river but as he crossed the winds blew fiercely, and the water rose, roaring in his ears as if he was crossing a storm in the wide ocean. The weight on his shoulders increased more and more until he thought he would go under. Holding on to his staff for support, he finally reached the other shore placing the child safely on the firm ground. "What have I carried? It could not have been heavier if it had been the whole world!" said Offerus. Then he heard the child's answer "You wished to serve me and I have chosen you as my servant. You have carried the king of the whole world. So that you may know who I am, please fix your staff on the ground." Offerus did as instructed. Out of the bare staff sprang leaves and clusters of dates. That is how Offerus knew that he had carried Christ. Thus he became Christopher, the Christ bearer.[21]

It is quite an amazing coincidence that Columbus should have in his name the evidence of the Holy Spirit, traditionally represented as a dove, and that he— Christopher—should have been entrusted to carry Christ across the Atlantic. Indeed, it is remarkable that his flagship should be the Santa Maria thus named after the Mother of God. That ship was bound to remain in the Americas. Columbus ordered it dismantled to build a small fort that he called Santa Trinidad (Holy Trinity) in honor of God Himself.

Symbolically, Columbus brought in Mary, Jesus, and the Holy Trinity to America and left them as a seed for the faith of future generations. A replica of St Luke's carved image of the Virgin Mother and Child went always with Columbus in his travels. After being buried for nearly seven-hundred years, the image of Our Lady of Guadalupe traveled in space and time from the original grave of St Luke in Thebes, to Constantinople, Rome, Seville, Guadalupe in Extremadura, and with Christopher Columbus to the newly discovered American continent. A great adventure of the faith was afoot.

---

[21] Please see: The Legend of Saint Christopher by Margaret Hodges, Eerdman's Books for Young Readers, Grand Rapids, Michigan, 2009.

The Native World

The New World that Columbus opened up to the Europeans was for many centuries cut off from the Old World. In 1492, Europe was entering the Modern Age, while the Americas were still for the most part in the Stone Age. Yet, the clash of those two big civilizations had such important implications that even today—five centuries later—there are many things we are struggling to understand.

Both the Aztec Empire in Mexico and the Inca Empire in Peru could not have existed without the high numbers of people needed to run such complex societies. There is an obvious difference between the population of the Americas at the time of the discovery and the low population density at the time of the arrival of the European settlers. Cortez and Pizarro conquered very large territories for Spain with small armies of just a few hundred men. Once the natives were subdued, the Spanish crown never needed a standing army to keep the peace. That peace lasted from the early 16th century to the American wars of independence that, for the most part, broke out in the 18th century. Until very recently, historians estimated rather low population figures for all of the Americas around the time of the discovery but that estimation is now being challenged. In all likelihood, we will never know the exact number; but a rough guess puts it at several dozen million, probably in the vicinity of one hundred million. That was approximately the population of Europe at the time.

How do we arrive at such numbers? First, we have two large empires, the Aztec Empire in Mexico and the Inca Empire in present-day Peru and Bolivia. We do not have exact population figures but we can calculate the approximate number of people needed to run those systems. As for the rest of the continent, countless tribes inhabited it. To the south and towards the north of Mexico, organized confederations were beginning to crop up, building enormous cities which disappeared a few decades after the Europeans first arrived. Again, the total number of inhabitants outside the organized empires is anyone's guess. Nevertheless, the low and high estimates seem to indicate that the population outside the organized entities was relatively high, perhaps comparable to their contemporary European populations. The fact remains that only a century or so after the discovery those populations had been nearly extinguished and entire cultures had disappeared from the face of the earth. How that came to pass is a fascinating mystery.

In his book *1491*, journalist Charles C. Mann writes: "Before it became the New World, the Western Hemisphere was vastly more populous and sophisticated than has been thought—an altogether more salubrious place to live at the time than, say, Europe. New evidence of both the extent of the population and its agricultural advancement leads to a remarkable conjecture: the Amazon rain forest may be largely a human artifact."[22]

To get an idea of how important the disappeared American civilizations were in the 16th century, we can take a look at the size and functionality of their cities. Tenochtitlan, the capital of the Aztec Empire, had running water and waste water systems. The streets were a model of cleanliness and tidiness maintained by a small force of organized workers. The citizens of Tenochtitlan lived in a much healthier and cleaner environment than did the king of France, whom centuries later had the Versailles palace built without a single toilet. In those years, for that matter, the world's biggest city was not Rome or Paris or London: it was Tenochtitlan and all over the continent there were—before the arrival of the Europeans—some huge cities. We are just beginning to discover some of those ruins: Cahokia, Calakmul, and many others.

Available to us there are reports by Hernan Cortez, Francisco Pizarro, and other explorers who got to see these vast empires in their last days. Many of them were astonished at the grandeur and vitality of these urban centers. Contrary to what is widely believed, the Spanish conquerors did not destroy these cities in order to seize their treasures. While certainly there was sacking and mistreatment, most damage done by Europeans was completely unintentional. Four centuries had to pass before scientists like Jenner and Pasteur created the science of microbiology so that we could understand the invisible forces that swept away America's indigenous nations.

The French explorer René Robert Sieur De La Salle left us a clue of what happened to some of those huge urban centers. He traveled in 1682 through the same Mississippi area that Hernando De Soto had explored a hundred years before. De Soto had not been able to establish a colony in that part of the world since it was "full of a large number of fenced villages and many well-trained archers."

A century later, La Salle found the ruins of those villages but they were no longer inhabited. The civilizations that had supported them just two generations before had vanished leaving the cities intact. De Soto had a chance to see a few cities like Cahokia from the relative safety of the rafts he used to explore the Mississippi. He saw the cities intact and active, packed with people and heavily guarded. What happened in the years following his visit is one of the saddest chapters in American history.

---

[22] *1491*, by Charles C. Mann, Vintage Books-Random House, New York, 2006.

The Century of Death

When Columbus left the island of Hispaniola in 1492, he also left one of his sailors who had fallen ill and died of the pox. The effect of European diseases on the American population was going to be monumentally more devastating than anything that could have affected the Europeans.

In the following years, the pigs that Hernando de Soto had left behind in Georgia, a French sailor suffering from viral hepatitis who was shipwrecked off the Massachusetts shores, and many other sources of infection added to Columbus' first visit, casting a dark mantle of pestilence and death which—according even to conservative estimations—annihilated nearly ninety percent of the American population.

Now there is evidence available of how the epidemic diseases spread from the Caribbean progressing in waves westward, northward and southward. Pestilence made the conquest of the Americas easier for the Europeans. When the conquest of America by the various European powers began, the Americas were practically defenseless, her warriors were dead long before they could offer any resistance to the invaders; many native nations perished entirely, others fell into irreversible social disorder. The survivors could not repel invaders that were technologically superior and also unwittingly carried deadly diseases for which the natives had no natural immunity.

When Francisco Pizarro reached Cajamarca in Peru in the year of 1531, a pox epidemic had already swept through the Inca Empire, killing approximately twenty percent of the population in a few years. There are strong reasons to believe this was a consequence of the Europeans arriving in 1492.

Among the victims were Huayno Capac, the Inca and his heir Ninan Coyuchui. The resulting power vacuum brought about a civil war between Atahualpa and Huascar —both likely heirs to the throne—adding to the hardships of the population that had barely survived the plague. Just a few days after overcoming his enemies and consolidating the kingdom's peace, Atahualpa learned about Pizarro's landing. By December of 1531, the Incas no longer ruled their vast empire. The end came rapidly to those civilizations that had thrived in South America for so many centuries. At their height, they ruled from Ecuador to the south of Chile, from the Peruvian shores of the Pacific to the edge of the great Amazonian basin in what is now Bolivia and Brazil.

Had it not been for the diseases, which weakened all of the American societies without exception, the conquest of America would have been as impossible as the full conquest of China or Japan. History would have been entirely different. The second wave of Europeans who would eventually settle down in America could do so because the native societies had been undermined by successive epidemics of smallpox, diphtheria, influenza, and other maladies brought by the first wave of European explorers. The original population of the Americas was indeed much higher before the discovery.

In December 1531—when Pizarro was consolidating the conquest of Peru—at the other end of the American continent, the bishop of Mexico got a surprising report: The Virgin Mary had appeared to a modest native called Juan Diego Cuauhtlatoatzin on Tepeyac hill near Tenochtitlan. A series of remarkable miracles confirmed the apparition. This miracle was followed by thousands of conversions among the natives and about nine million American Christians were received into the Church in the years to follow. The conversions span the territories extending from California to the shores of the Gulf of Mexico. Thus began the evangelization of America guided by Mary of Nazareth.

When the English settlers came to Massachusetts in 1620, they found the coastal aboriginal tribes depopulated by the plague. That was probably viral hepatitis caught from a Frenchman that survived a shipwreck off the coast of Cape Cod and was rescued by the natives. That was a small example of the devastation that European diseases had brought on the ancient Native American world. A new age was dawning on the Americas as the ancient native nations faded into oblivion, fatally wounded by foreign diseases.

The Blood of Sacrifices

Let us leave for a moment this year of 1531, which ends with the conquest of Peru and the apparition of the Virgin Mary in Mexico. We shall go back to the year of 1398, one hundred and thirty years before the Virgin's apparition on Tepeyac Hill. In that particular year, a child was born who was destined to be prominent in the history of the Aztecs. Someone unknown to many of us but very important in the history of pre-Columbian Mexico: Tlecaellel, the architect of the Aztec empire. He dedicated the last reconstruction of the High Temple in Tenochtitlan; Tlecaellel brought the Aztec nation to the height of its power. The High Temple was dedicated in 1484 with a high number of human sacrifices. The Aztec historian Quauhtlehuanitzin says about him:

"There were many great, awe-inspiring kings and warriors among those peoples, near and far and all over the world. But the most courageous and distinguished of them all in the nation was the great captain, the great warrior Tlecaellel. It was he who ordered the worship of the Huitzilopochtli, the demon god of the Mexicas."

Tlecaellel was the organizer and founder of the Aztec empire that Cortez would discover a hundred years later. Tlecaellel lived for almost a century and during that period of time, he implemented a master plan to strengthen the power of the Aztec emperors among the peoples in the region. He himself refused to be an emperor and chose instead to be the power behind the throne. He turned down the proposal to be a crowned king by saying: "I am already a king." In promoting a large number of sacrifices to the demon Huitzilopochtli, he set off a series of regional wars with the only purpose of capturing victims for the sacrifices he would offer up "like hot bread fresh from the oven, soft and delicious." At the age of thirty-one in 1429, he emerged as a mighty military leader and appointed the three kings of the Triple Alliance by his own power. Indeed, he was the empire's true ruler for seventy-seven years.

Perhaps the most macabre time in the macabre life of Tlecaellel occurred in 1487 when he was eighty-nine years old. In that year, the great pyramidal temple of Huitzilopochtli was built right in central Tenochtitlan, a striking one-hundred ft. high building, containing a large complex full of apartments, corridors, and sanctuaries where the god's priests lived and worked. The two main "gods" in the Aztec pantheon – to whom most human sacrifices were made – were Huitzilopochtli and Tezcatlipoca. Its 'priests' would paint their bodies black; their permanently uncut hair was always plastered with dry blood. Their sharp teeth tapered to a point. The new temple was erected and dedicated by order of Tlecaellel who decided, for that special event, to offer up the greatest sacrifice of human lives ever made in the empire's history. Summing up the various accounts of that sad day, historian R. C. Padden described it as follows:

"Well before daybreak, legionnaires prepared the victims, who were put in close single file down the steps of the great pyramid, through the city, out over the causeways, and as far as the eye could see. For the average person viewing the spectacle from his rooftop, it would appear that the victims stretched in lines to the ends of the earth. The bulk of the unfortunates were from hostile provinces and the swollen ranks of slavery. On the pyramid summit four slabs had been set up, one at the head of each staircase, for Tlecaellel and the three kings of the Aztec Triple Alliance, all of them were to begin the affair as sacrificial priests.

All were in readiness; the lines of victims were strung out for miles, milling about like cattle, waiting their turn in the line that was about to move. Suddenly, the brilliantly arrayed Kings appeared on the platform and silence fell all over the city. Together they approached Huitzilopochtli's chapel and made reverent obeisance. As they turned to join their aides at the four slabs, great snakeskin drums began to throb, announcing that the lines could now begin to move."[23]

The victims were readily arranged on the altar where the priest would tear their hearts out by quickly striking them with a huge obsidian knife. The operation was quick and accurate. Once the victims were sacrificed, they were sent tumbling down the steps where the assistants would quarter the bodies that would be cooked and eaten later.

---

[23] *The Hummingbird and the Hawk: Conquest and Sovereignty in the Valley of Mexico* 1503-1541, by R. C. Padden, Torchbooks Paperback, 1970.

The ceremony went on for four days and we know that at least 80,000 individuals were sacrificed. Tlecaellel ordered that the event should be seen by all of the noblemen and their families. Horrified by that sight, most of them ran away in terror but although they could escape such horror, they could not escape the nauseating smell of human blood engulfing the entire city. The 1487 massacre is one of the appalling chapters in the long list of horrors that is the history of man.

Save Us from Those Who Devour Us

What the participants and the hopeless victims in that massacre did not know was that that evil social order was soon to change forever. Before that sad generation was gone, the whole nation would be rescued by Christ's love by means of very unprecedented, amazing events.

"They devour my people as they devour bread; they do not call upon the Lord." The phrase taken from Psalm 14 can be used to understand how God dealt with the anguish of the poor and downtrodden American peoples. God's grace was to be dispensed to them in a way never seen before. Such grace came down especially on the poor Mexican natives truly like a refreshing rain. In those days, in the small town of Cuautitlan, not very far from Tenochtitlan there lived a little boy of about thirteen years of age. By then, he was an apprentice tilma weaver. Tilmas are the traditional fiber ponchos typical among the Chichimeca people; he was a Macehualtin, a commoner. He is likely to have attended the sacrifices on that horrible day, maybe out of youthful curiosity. His name was Cuauhtlatouac, "the one who speaks like an eagle."

Some forty years later, Cuauhtlatouac was baptized with the Christian name of Juan Diego. The Mother of God appeared to him on Tepeyac Hill right where the Aztec goddess Toniatzin was worshiped in ancient days. In another of those remarkable coincidences in history, the apparition gave rise to the Mexican devotion to Our Lady of Guadalupe. Columbus had already given that name to one of the Caribbean islands, in appreciation of Our Lady for having helped him survive a shipwreck. Columbus was honoring not the Mexican advocation[24]—that would develop four decades later—but the

---

[24] **Advocation.** Lat. *advocatio, advocationis, advocare.* **1.** Guardianship, protection or patronage of God or of the saints to the community or institution that takes its name. **2.** Complementary denomination that is applied to the name of a divine or holy person and that refers to a certain mystery, virtue or attribute, to special moments of his/her life, to places linked to his/her presence or to the finding of his/her image; i.e., Christ Lord of Mercy, Our Lady of Hope, Our Lady of Fatima. **3.** Denomination of the corresponding images, of the sanctuaries and days in which they are venerated, of the entities under their patronage, etc. **4.** Advocacy: protection or special dedication. ‖ It is important to notice that by choosing to appear in Mexico and in Extremadura under the same advocation, Our

original devotion from the town of Guadalupe in Extremadura, Spain.

While the Tlecaellel generation was exceedingly bloodthirsty, the Aztecs were not the only ones that made use of human sacrifices to terrify people and to worship their gods. Evidence of human sacrifices among the cultures of the high Andean plateau has been found also.

Other peoples on the continent practiced cannibalism and ritual homosexuality at different times in history. In my view, the horror of the poor slaves and prisoners is unimaginable. The remains of sacrificed children in the Inca Empire fill us with sadness and indignation. Because of those unnatural acts, divine punishment fell upon these peoples when least expected. God stepped into the Americas as described by the Prophet Habakkuk, preceded by pestilence and death, melting the mountains with his might, crushing the wicked forever.[25]

Not all was punishment and destruction. After the fall of the Aztec Empire, the "one that speaks like an eagle" Juan Diego Cuauhtlatoatzin was selected by Heaven to bring to the good people of his race a life-giving vision of peace that would endure through the ages all the way to our days.

Lady seems to be pointing to her intention to unite the two nations under her special protection and patronage. That may be an indication, a model of what Our Lady plans to do with all the human race in the future.

[25] Habakkuk 3.

2
THE EAGLE AND THE SERPENT

In Genesis, we read that God made man in his "image and likeness." From the beginning, the human race has tried to understand the Universe using the most basic tool of our intellect, our ability to compare. The Spanish conquerors of Mexico were still medieval men and shared many concepts and beliefs with the Stone Age warriors they encountered in the Americas. The ancient settlers of the New World had parted ways with the cultures of Europe and Asia before the wheel was invented, before the horse was domesticated, even before man began to master agriculture in the fertile crescent of the Middle East. Native Americans and Europeans shared a common humanity and many ancestral beliefs. They had arrived at those beliefs through different routes and now they were face to face, unwittingly trying to recognize something of themselves in each other.

Metaphorical contemplation is a form of understanding; we learn to think by comparing things. Human intelligence thrives in all kinds of comparisons and most times we are not aware of that constant stream of "like and not-like" operations flowing through our thoughts, our actions, and our language.

The very roots of the word "intelligence" point to a comparison. The Latin word *intelligentia* derives from *inteligere* a verb composed of two parts: *intus* meaning "among" and *legere* meaning "to select." The very origin of the word makes reference to comparing two things finding them sometimes similar, sometimes dissimilar. Humans are, to various degrees, masters in the art of finding analogies and expressing through metaphors. Our intellectual experience rests mainly on finding "the likeness of unlike things" to use Richard Mulcaster's brilliant phrase. Please join me as we conduct a short exercise: comparing the image and likeness of two cultures that were not alike at all.

Since 1531, Our Lady of Guadalupe has been a constant mystery. Someone who is at the same time woman and sign, Guadalupe is the encounter and union between two races. She is the origin of a new identity for both the Spanish and Mexican people. In her two different cosmogonies meet, two continents are united; two races are melted into a new race. Our Lady of Guadalupe—in her Spanish and her Mexican advocations—appears at a climactic time in history when Spain, a former Roman province, begins to find its identity as a nation following a centuries-old struggle with invaders after the collapse of the Roman Empire.

Both the Spaniards and the Mexicans of the 16th century were moved by a spiritual fervor that modern man could hardly understand. Those two cultures had enormous differences but also surprisingly great similarities. Finding the likeness between these two unlike peoples would have been impossible by human means but a supernatural event made the fusion of both groups possible. The story forms a wonderful parable taught to every generation from the humble *ayate*[26] of San Juan Diego.

All the pre-Columbian nations in the Americas had mystical preoccupations and so did the Spaniards. The native world was filled with gods haunting the imagination of the ancient Americans. The image imprinted on San Juan Diego's tilma contains many signs that the natives could read like a book. In that book specifically prepared for their imagination, Our Lady of Guadalupe gave counsel, consolation, faith in the future, and a strong national identity to a broken and long-suffering nation oppressed by violence and death.

Our Lady of Guadalupe had been a witness to the fall of the pagan Roman Empire. Later she witnessed the fall of Muslim Spain at the end of the Spanish Reconquest. When no one knew that the Modern Age was just starting, she took Mexico from the Stone Age to Modernity in one single generation; and she moved Spain from being a backward corner of Europe to be a worldwide empire.

Obviously we cannot devote this book to compare the whole of the Spanish and Aztec cultures as they stood in the early 16th century; instead, we will concentrate on certain details that will be very useful later to understand the message delivered by Our Lady of Guadalupe to Juan Diego and his contemporaries. Like a diamond that assumes different colors and shapes as light hits its many facets, the message of Our Lady of Guadalupe presents itself to many cultures, revealing the same truths with force and precision. In my understanding that is a hidden miracle, perhaps one of the greatest ever performed by the Virgin Mary.[27]

---

[26] **Ayate**, from the Nahuatl word *ayatl*, is a cloth made from the fiber of the maguey plant. The word is also used for a cloak or poncho garment made from that kind of cloth. In this case, the words *ayate* and *tilma* are synonymous.

[27] "I thank you, Father, Lord of Heaven and Earth, that you have concealed these things from the wise and understanding and revealed them to little children; yes, Father, for so it pleased you well." Such are the thoughts of Jesus expressed in Luke 10:21. The most extraordinary private revelations of our age have been given to the humblest messengers at Guadalupe de Extremadura, Fatima, Lourdes, La Salette, and Tepeyac. Our Lady of Guadalupe could have easily appeared to Bishop Zumárraga but it "pleased God so well" that a humble and despised

The Mythical Foundation of Tenochtitlan

There are many different versions of the foundation of Tenochtitlan although one can gather some essential symbolic elements. We are interested in looking at the images transmitted from generation to generation. The truth about the foundation of the great city of Tenochtitlan or the real story of Quetzalcoatl will never be known for certain but we are not looking for a mere chronicle; we want to enter to the extent possible into the mind of a unique nation. Mexico participated in a real clash of civilizations; knowing how they formulated their myths will give us valuable insight on how the miraculous image of Guadalupe was able to communicate with the people of Mexico with such effectiveness and immediacy.

In general, the story begins in Aztlan, the ancestral land of the Mexica people. There various hostile groups surrounded them. Copil, the adult son of a sorceress learns from his mother that the demon Huitzilopochtli had disrespected her gravely. Copil promised to avenge that offense. Copil knew that the Mexica warriors—the people of Huitzilopochtli—were congregated in the heights of Chapultepec and so he began to discredit them maliciously with the surrounding nations breeding distrust among them.

Giving credit to the words of Copil the neighboring tribes began to prepare for war with the object of exterminating the Mexicas. Copil proceeded to climb to a hill near a lake to watch from there the destruction of his enemies. While he was there Huitzilopochtli, very indignant, called his priests and told them to go to that hill where they would find Copil the traitor waiting patiently for the destruction of the Mexicas. The priests ambushed the traitor, killed him and extracted his heart that was later presented to Huitzilopochtli. The god then ordered one of his servants to throw the heart of his perfidious enemy in the lake. The priests did so and from that moment a cactus grew from the thorny heart of Copil.[28]

The *Crónica Mexicana* by Hernando de Alvarado Tezozomoc[29] tells the same story somewhat differently: the Mexicas arrived at a new land persuaded by the demon Huitzilopochtli. They found a mound of stones covered by a cactus forest. At its base, they found an anthill and above the hill, they saw a royal eagle holding a snake in its claws and devouring it.

Archaeologists have established that Mexico was inhabited before the arrival of the Mexicas by peoples that colonized the area of Tlatelolco north

---

Commoner was the witness of such a great event.

[28] *Arqueología Mexicana, El Mito de la Fundación de México Tenochtitlan*; Especial 62, and *El Cactus en México Catálogo Visual* by Enrique Vela, June 2015.

[29] *Crónica Mexicana by Hernando de Alvarado Tezozomoc*. SEP, México, D.F. 1943, Colección Biblioteca Enciclopédica Popular, vol. 33. Selection and introduction by Mario Mariscal.

of Tenochtitlan. When the Mexicas arrived they conquered the territories around the valley, gradually draining vast marsh areas they settled and exploited. Tenochtitlan eventually became a city-state forming a powerful alliance with Texcoco and Tlacopan.

The Mexicas grew powerful in that unassailable place deftly maintaining control over the surrounding populations. In their view, the sun god was blessing them by being reborn every day.

To this day, the eagle above the cactus holding the serpent is the most enduring symbol of Mexico. The eagle represents the rising sun while the serpent—formerly the symbol of the wisdom of Quetzalcoatl—became a symbol of evil. The new Christian destiny of the ancient nation was changed to fight on the side of good against evil.

A Brief Who's Who of Aztec Mythology

Like most other inhabitants of the ancient Americas, the Aztecs had a dualistic solar religion. Their sun god Tonatiuhteotl rose every morning mounted on the high flying eagle Cuauhxicalli after being reborn from the womb of Mother Earth, Coatlicue Toniatzin, also known as Teteohinnan, the Mother of the Gods.

The rising of the sun was understood as a struggle between two warriors: the sun god, and his opposer the ruler of darkness. These two warrior gods were brothers in constant combat. Their sister Coyolxauhqui, the moon goddess was depicted decapitated and dismembered. In that way, the phases of the moon were explained as the gradual dismembering of the goddess by her enemy the sun, who vanquished the rulers of darkness every morning.

The Aztec pantheon also included Tlaloc the god of rain, thunder, hail, and clouds. Tlaloc was on the side of life with the sun. Tezcatlipoca and Coyolxauhqui were on the side of death and darkness. Among their allies was Huitzilopochtli the demon ruler of the underworld.

Mother earth Coatlicue, the mother of all the gods, was the giver of life and also the one destined to receive the dead. It is important to examine how they were represented to their worshipers. The images of the gods had many attributes that later appeared in the image of Our Lady of Guadalupe to help the natives understand their new Christian mother and to draw them closer to Christ.

A Battle between Light and Darkness

The Aztecs understood the universe as cycles that complemented each other. The cycle of the day was a battle between the forces of light and darkness. Humans needed to help the forces of light, making sure that the sun god had enough soldiers to win the battle and rise again the next morning. If the sun was defeated and darkness triumphed then the night would be eternal and mankind would perish. Mankind's role in this battle was to provide warriors for the army of the sun god to perpetuate the cycle.

The hearts of the sacrificed warriors were placed in stone vessels and offered to the gods. The offerings for the sun were placed in the Cuauhxicalli, a vase that had the shape of an eagle with its eyes made to resemble sun rays. The eagle took the warriors up to the realm of the sun to help him in battle. In the same manner, there was also a vessel for the god of darkness made in the shape of a jaguar, the nocturnal hunter Ocelotl Cuauhxicalli. The spots in the jaguar's coat represented the stars at night. The tension between opposites light and darkness, warm and cold, near and far, east and west, winter and summer was considered essential for the existence of life. That is what the Aztecs learned from observing nature.

The rising of the sun over the horizon gave the Aztecs the idea that the Earth was giving birth to the god of light who then chased darkness out of the sky going to rest at night, feeding on the sacrifices so it could rise again to battle one more day. Coatlicue the earth was the beginning and the end of the gods; from the womb of the earth they went forth into battle and returned there to rest from combat.

Tonatiuh the Rising Sun

The sun god Tonatiuh also called Tonatiuhteotl, demanded daily human sacrifices. If those were lacking, the sun could hide permanently, leaving mankind in darkness. Two human hearts per day were required to feed the sun after the daily battle. In the Solar Stone, commonly known as the Aztec Calendar, the sun is represented with a sacrificial knife coming out of his mouth. Behind his face, a red solar disk is shining.

Coatlicue Toniatzin, Mother Earth

Coatlicue Toniatzin was often represented with her head cut off. Her arms are two snakes; she has the legs of an eagle because she is the mother of the sun. Her umbilical cord is shown feeding the ground from where all living things come. Her dress is made of snakes. Coatlicue means, "the one dressed in a skirt made of snakes." In the Aztec conception of the world, everything living is made of snakes.[30]

The snakes tied in a bow along with her skull buckle indicate that Coatlicue Toniatzin is pregnant. The skull indicates death, the sure destiny of every living thing. She is depicted with plentiful breasts, a sign of fertility and the motherly generosity of earth. Coatlicue gives and takes life. She is the mother of all 402 gods. She completes the total of 403 gods, a number that is 13 times 31. The number thirteen appears often in Aztec mythology: there are

---

[30] I wonder (jokingly) if that should be considered a very early intuition of the modern string theory now so popular among theoretical physicists. A string closely resembles a snake and vice versa.

thirteen heavens and nine underworlds. This representation is one of the major meanings of the number thirteen. The Aztecs counted thirteen major articulations in the human body, thirteen rectangles on a turtle shell and thirteen rings on the tail of the sacred rattlesnake. For that reason, the Pleiades constellation is also called "the tail of the rattlesnake." The Aztec calendar of two hundred and sixty days was divided in twenty months of thirteen days.

Tlaloc the God of Rain

Tlaloc is the god of rain, hail, lightning, thunder or any other thing that comes from above. He is dressed with the wind, symbolized by feathers. His dress has blue and white stripes signifying the sky and the clouds bringing rain. Tlaloc is a companion of the sun god because in agricultural societies sun and rain are essential to life.[31]

Huitzilopochtli

The demon Huitzilopochtli, "the left-handed hummingbird" or "southern hummingbird" is one of the dead warriors who inhabit the Paradise of the Sun in the east where he sips the blood from the "precious flowers" – the hearts of the sacrificed victims of the flower wars. The final part of his name opochtli is used to refer to the nahual or other self. He is the last son of Coatlicue, mother earth. The Franciscan historian Bernardino de Sahagun believes that the name of this deity reveals the idea of a purely demonic character, the fallen angel that requested the human sacrifices.[32] His adversary was the god Tlaloc, god of rain.

Tezcatlipoca

Tezcatlipoca, the Lord of the Night Winds, is the god of fate and darkness. His name in Nahuatl means, "smoking mirror" and he was one of the most feared gods. He was related to the forces of evil and destruction. He was the patron god of witchcraft, divination, and black magic. He was represented with soot mixed with light reflecting metal, dressed as a jaguar with an obsidian-pointed spear. He is the god of war and violence, the adversary of Quetzalcoatl.

Tezcatlipoca demanded complete subservience even from those in the noblest echelons of Aztec society all the way to the highest position of Aztec nobility. The king had to stand utterly naked in front of that god to repeat a

---

[31] *Our Lady of Guadalupe and the Miracle of the Roses* lecture given by Luis Fernando Castaneda Monter at Saint Francis Chapel; Prudential Center, Boston, 2013.

[32] *The Florentine Codex: General History of the Things of New Spain*, by Bernardino de Sahagun; translated by Arthur J. O. Anderson and Charles E. Dibble; University of Utah Press, 2002.

formulated prayer: "O master, O our lord, O lord of the near, of the far, O night, O wind ... Poor am I. In what manner shall I act for your city? In what manner shall I act for the governed, for the lowly Commoner? For I am blind, I am deaf, I am an imbecile, and in excrement, in filth hath my lifetime been ... Perhaps you did mistake me for another; perhaps you seekest another in my stead."[33] The description of Tezcatlipoca fits very well with the Christian idea of God's enemy, the devil.

Quetzalcoatl the Precious Twin

Quetzalcoatl is the Aztec god of agriculture; he was represented as a feathered serpent associated with Venus the evening star. Many historians believe that Quetzalcoatl was a person who was later deified and incorporated into the Aztec, Toltec, and Mayan pantheon. The myth describes him as a bearded man of white skin who came to Yucatan from the east. He gave the peoples of Mexico the knowledge of agriculture, metalwork, the arts, astronomy, and the calendar. He rejected human sacrifices and taught a religion of love and peace. Quetzalcoatl was considered the rival of Tezcatlipoca, the god of darkness. In Aztec mythology, he was also opposed by Huitzilopochtli, the Left-handed Hummingbird, the god of war.

Prophecies, Miracles, and Dreams

According to legend, those evil gods had sent Quetzalcoatl into exile. Before leaving, he promised to return at the end of the age on a certain day and end all human sacrifices. The prophecy proved to be instrumental at the time of the conquest of Mexico by the Spaniards. According to prominent Catholic author Warren H. Carroll, author of Our Lady of Guadalupe and the Conquest of Darkness: "The wise men of Mexico had expected that the returning Quetzalcoatl would land not only in his name year, 1-reed but also on his personal name day, called in their calendar 9-wind. Good Friday, April 22, 1519, was a 9-wind day in a 1-reed year. As a priest, Ce Acal Topiltzin Quetzalcoatl wore black. Cortez landing this day was dressed in black for the commemoration of Good Friday."[34]

---

[33] *Mexico: From the Olmecs to the Aztecs—Ancient Peoples and Places* by Michael D. Coe and Rex Koontz, published by Thames and Hudson. Notice the similarity of the formula to show utter self-humiliation before the false god with the way St Juan Diego Cuauhtlatoatzin responds to the Virgin Mary on his fourth encounter at Tepeyac.

[34] *Apéndice – Explicación del Códice Geroglífico de Mr. Aubin de Historia de las Indias de la Nueva España y Islas de Tierra Firme*, by Diego Duran and Alfredo Chavero; II, p 71, 1880. It is remarkable that Ce Acal Topiltzin Quetzalcoatl according to some legends was born on May 13 A.D. 895—a date coinciding with the first apparition of Our Lady of Fatima: May 13, 1917. Such coincidences occur throughout the history of Marian apparitions.

Franciscan missionary Bernardino de Sahagun infroms us that the Aztecs firmly believed Quetzalcoatl would return one day. Who was Quetzalcoatl? We can only speculate that he was a man who had the most extraordinary influence in the ancient cultures of Mexico. There are many accounts of his appearance but most of the legends agree that he arrived first in the Yucatan peninsula from the East. The name the Maya gave him, Kukulcan suggests a Celtic name like that of the Irish mythical hero Cú Chulainn. The Aztec depictions of Quetzalcoatl are of a bearded man with Caucasian features rather Germanic in appearance. He is represented symbolically as a feathered serpent. The feathers represent the wind in Aztec iconography suggesting that Quetzalcoatl is a flying serpent or a wind god. He appears in history at some point around the 10th century. He is presented as a compassionate man, always willing to help the needy. He taught the natives agriculture and how to build cities; he also gave them a religion emphasizing the service of others, peace, love, and contentment. Once his civilizing mission was completed he built a ship and left sailing eastward. Before leaving, he prophesied that one future day white bearded men just like him, the sons of the sun god, would come and conquer the land, bringing great prosperity and progress.[35]

The Prophecy of Papantzin

Princess Papantzin was the sister of Emperor Moctezuma. She was given in marriage to the king of Tlatelolco but the king soon died and Papantzin returned to live with his family in the imperial palace. Around 1509, she fell gravely ill and died. She was laid to rest in the palace garden. Her mother found Papantzin alive the day after her burial. Once the commotion caused by her apparent resurrection subsided, Papantzin told her brother and family about her extraordinary experience. She told them that a while after her apparent death she gradually came back to her senses. She found herself on the shore of a wide river. On one side of that river, there were piles of skulls and she could hear them cry and scream but was unable to understand what they were saying. On the opposite side of the river, she saw gathering a growing number of bearded men with white skin. As she was trying to cross the river a beautiful young man appeared. He was enveloped in light brighter than the sun, he had two large wings on his back and his right hand carried a cross. That messenger kindly told her that the skulls represented her ancestors while the bearded white men were the sons of the sun preparing to sail the wide waters to conquer the Mexican Empire, adding that their time to cross the wide waters was still in the future.

---

[35] *Mujeres Célebres de México* by Carlos Hernandez, pp. 16-17, Casa Editorial Lozano, San Antonio, Texas, 1918.

Signs in the Heavens

Moctezuma listened to the account of that vision with a fearful heart. He understood that the ancient prophecy of Quetzalcoatl was about to be fulfilled during his reign. Since he was sitting on the Throne of the Feathered Serpent, he knew he had to relinquish it when Quetzalcoatl arrived to rightfully claim it back. The anxiety in the heart of Moctezuma caused by Papantzin's vision diminished as the years went by uneventfully. The daily sacrifices and the flower wars continued without interruption until one day in 1510—without any warning or seismic movement—the Lake Texcoco was moved violently out of the lakebed causing great damage and many deaths in the coastal villages. Not long after that strange event, a comet appeared in the night sky.[36] In 1516 a second comet appeared, and then a third one followed by a strong earthquake. Those were bad omens for Emperor Moctezuma and his gods; three times a sun had dared to cross the sky as the gods of darkness watched impotently. Finally, even the Coatlicue, the Earth mother of all gods was trembling. The Emperor of Mexico was no longer anxious or uneasy, he was now in full panic: it was clear to him that the gods were coming to reclaim his throne.

The Day of Reckoning

Moctezuma called to court all the wise counselors, astrologers, and shamans of Mexico. All subjects were told to report any extraordinary dream, vision, or omen. The Emperor wanted to find peace by decoding the arcane messages reaching his anxious heart. Many were summoned and asked to produce a solution. Some of them were sent to perish in the royal prisons while others were sacrificed to appease the gods. While still in darkness about the time and mode of the disgrace the gods were bringing upon his realm, Moctezuma's guards presented him with a man, he was old and had no ears or toes. The humble man informed the Emperor not about dreams or visions but about mountains moving about the sea near Yucatan. Warriors and priests were sent without delay to verify the old man's report. They came back promptly with even more disturbing information: large ships were anchored near the coast; bearded white men were setting up camp and fishing. It was Good Friday, April 22, 1519; as predicted that was a 9-wind day in a 1-reed year. A beautiful Mexican full moon illuminated the night sky above the kingdom of the Left-handed Hummingbird but nothing could dispel the dark forebodings in the

---

[36] *The Codex Telleriano-Remensis* (Manuscript Mexicain No. 385) depicted "an immense streamer of light leaping from the Earth to the stars connecting to the Spanish calendar in 1509 A.D." *La Vie Quotidienne des Aztèques a la Veille de la Conquête Espagnole* by Jacques Soustelle. Hachette Littératures; Paris, 1955. Halley's Comet was also visible in 1531, in the year when Our Lady of Guadalupe appeared to Juan Diego Cuauhtlatoatzin.

Emperor's heart. When Moctezuma summoned the original informer to give him the royal reward, the old man had vanished. He was nowhere to be found. The sons of the sun god had entered the realm of Huitzilopochtli. The dreaded time of the end was at hand.

Princess Papantzin was perhaps the first to understand that the mission of the Spaniards was supernaturally ordered. She took some time to consider the new religion of the conquerors, moved no doubt by the force of her vision. She eventually realized that she was the first person of her race to see the Cross of Christ in the hands of the messenger angel. She humbly received Christian instruction and was the first woman in the nation to be baptized, taking the name of Doña Maria Papantzin.

3

THE ASCENT OF SPAIN

The Spanish conquerors came upon Moctezuma's Empire like divine punishment for the unnatural cruelty of the Aztec practices. The imagery of the Prayer of Habakkuk comes to mind: cruel oppressors that devour the poor, a God of light and justice swiftly liberating the oppressed, riding horses over the churning waters of the sea; those are all images quite apropos to describe the arrival of the conquerors.[37]

Who were those few brave Spanish men who dared to capture a vast organized empire of warriors, well equipped to resist any invasion, ruthlessly ruling over several million subjects, many of them eager to die in battle for their Emperor?

To know who they were, we must go back in time to pre-Roman Spain. In pre-Roman times, numerous tribes populated the Iberian Peninsula. Their origins are lost in the mist of prehistory. Carthaginians and Greeks had settled the Mediterranean coast; Celtic tribes inhabited the coast of Portugal and Galicia. In the two centuries before Christ, the Romans conquered Spain and colonized it but the conquest was not easy; the northern regions remained unstable and rebellious domains. The Celts proved to be a headache for the Roman conquerors. The resistance in the region now known as Catalonia was so fierce that the Roman historian Livius called them ferox genus, the "fierce people."[38] About one hundred years before the death of Christ, the Romans managed to pacify most of the region but the tribes of Asturias and Cantabria were still resisting well into the first century.

When the Empire collapsed, various barbarian tribes coming from the

---

[37] Habakkuk 3:1-15.

[38] *Breve Historia de España* by Henry Kamen, p. 9; translation by Marta Hernández Salván, Barcelona, Spain, 2009. The Romans called the region of modern Catalonia, Hispania Citerior. Towards the first century, they were called Tarraconensis, for their capital was Tarraco, that is modern Tarragona.

steppes of Central Asia began to invade Roman territory. In the 3rd century, Roman Hispania was attacked frequently from France and Africa. In 409 A.D. several Germanic tribes arrived crossing the Pyrenees. Eventually, one tribe, the Visigoths prevailed over the rest and were able to establish a kingdom that lasted until the 8th century. In 710 after the death of the Visigoth king Witiza, his descendants were not allowed to inherit the throne of Toledo so they endeavored to seize power by force by allying with the Moors. They solicited the help of the ruler of Muslim North Africa, Musa ibn Nusayr, to fight newly elected King Roderic. In the spring of 711, Moroccan General Tarik ibn Ziyad crossed the strait into Spain. King Roderic alone presented battle to superior forces and was killed in Guadalete.[39]

The Muslim forces moved to take Toledo, gaining control of the Visigoth Kingdom. About a decade later Pelayo,[40] King of Asturias began the Christian resistance at the Battle of Covadonga. The Reconquest—the long war against the Muslim occupation—was going to last nearly eight centuries until the fall of Granada to Christian forces in 1492.

Spain was for centuries a crucible where great soldiers were formed. When the Spaniards could finally expel the Moors from their territory, the economy in the peninsula was in shambles after centuries of bleeding life and treasure in countless battles. The Christians of Spain learned through suffering that they had to stick together and they had to be good fighters if they expected to survive. They were no longer Romans but they preserved their Roman Catholic faith after fighting the Arians first, and the Muslims later. Through those centuries of war, the Church in Spain produced many of the greatest Christian saints of the age.

St James the First to Evangelize Spain

The first to reach Spain with the Gospel of Jesus Christ was St James the Apostle. Tradition declares that James arrived in Asturias in the first century with his new disciples through Galicia, Castile, and Aragon, in the territory of Celtic Iberia, where the city of Zaragoza is located, by the River Ebro.[41]

There James preached for many days, finally choosing eight men as his companions, teaching them about the Kingdom of God and praying. On the 2nd day of January of A.D. 40, James was praying with his disciples by the River Ebro when he heard angels singing the words "Hail Mary full of grace;" then he saw a vision of Mary the Virgin Mother of Christ standing on a

---

[39] That is when news of the invasion reached Seville, prompting clergy to transport the relics of the Cathedral to a safer area to the north. At that time, they carried the image carved by St Luke and other sacred objects, burying them near the Guadalupe River in Extremadura. The relics remained there until the Virgin Mary revealed their location to Gil Cordero six centuries later.

[40] Pelagius.

[41] Also known as Saragossa.

marble pillar. The Virgin Mary, who was still living in Judea, asked James to build a church in that exact place. She also asked him to build the altar around the marble pillar where she was standing. She also promised that the altar would remain in that spot until the end of times so that God could work great portents and marvels through her intercession for those imploring her help.

When the vision ended, the pillar remained. St James and his disciples immediately began building a church in that place. Before the building was completed, St James chose a leader among his disciples, leaving the church to his care. What is now the Basilica de Nuestra Señora del Pilar was the first temple ever dedicated to the Virgin Mary. When St James died a martyr's death in Jerusalem, his disciples took his remains to Spain. He was buried in Compostela (*Gael.* "Field of Stars") that is now called Santiago de Compostela (Santiago, *Gael.* "Saint James") in the region of Galicia. From the very beginnings of the faith, Spain was forever under a special Marian patronage.

Through long centuries of strife and war, a race was forged. The Spanish hidalgos found their identity as Christian knights always under the protection of Mary Most Holy. One day great saints, great warriors, and great mariners would cross the globe spreading the faith of Christ under the Marian banner.

The Battle of Rio Salado

The campaign to recover Spain from the Moors was well underway by the time Gil Cordero had a vision of Our Lady of Guadalupe. The Christians were consolidating local alliances and a united country was emerging—a country under the faith of the Cross—united in purpose to free the land for Christ. Christian Spain was destined to be one, great, and free.

By 1212, the Muslims were rapidly losing control of the Peninsula to the Christians. After a resounding Christian victory in the Battle of Las Navas de Tolosa on July 16, 1212, Muslim territorial unity in Spain collapsed.

Previously in 1195, the Christians had suffered a painful defeat before the Moors at the Battle of Alarcos. After that, Pope Innocent III proclaimed a crusade against the Muslims. Urged by the Papal Bull, many among the Franks and the Knights Templars came to the aid of the Spanish cause. The combined Christian armies consisted of Aragon, Castile, Portugal, and a sizable number of foreign Catholic Crusaders. For the final expedition, the army of Navarre joined the Christian forces while the Franks and other foreigners left, discouraged by the harsh peninsular weather.

The Christian army—now wholly Spanish and Portuguese—moved to take the citadel of Castroferral. They could not advance beyond the hills; the passes were well guarded by Muslim forces. Through providential intervention, a local shepherd directed them to a pass where the army could cross safely and the Christian army took advantage of the priceless information and marched on. The Christians completely defeated the Muslims on July 16, 1212, at Las Navas de Tolosa with the citadels of Baeza and Ubeda falling to the Christian forces soon after. That defeat was the beginning of the end for the Mohammedan domination in Spain.

Only one Muslim kingdom survived in Granada. Towards the end of the 13th century, the Marinid, a new Sunni Muslim dynasty, emerged in Africa. After a series of sea and land victories against the Spaniards, the Marinid gathered a formidable invasion force to retake Spain once and for all. Knowing very well what was coming upon him, King Alfonso XI decided to ask his father-in-law Alfonso IV of Portugal for help. He did not want to repeat the mistakes made by King Roderic in 711. The fate of the whole peninsula was at stake. He sent his wife Queen Mary to ask for and secure the help of her father Alfonso IV of Portugal. After some rather serious differences were ironed out, the King of Portugal joined the King of Castile in the struggle against this second Muslim invasion.

The Christian troops met the Moors at Rio Salado, Cadiz on the 30th day of October 1340. The troops of the King of Morocco, Abu el Hassan, and the army of Yusuf I of Granada were on the Muslim side. Across the river, the troops of Alfonso XI of Castile, Alfonso IV King of Portugal, and the armies of the Crown of Aragon were ready to present battle.

The Marinid fought without armor while the Christian's cavalry, soldiers, and horses were well protected with shields and coats of mail. The Spaniards were outnumbered three to one but they were more experienced fighters, and they had a technological edge: their armor. The combined Christian forces 22,000 strong faced well over 60,000 Muslim troops. The Spanish and Portuguese kings trusted the fight to God by the intercession of Mary Most Holy. The Muslims were defeated.

The king of Portugal earned that day the title of "El Bravo," having charged daringly and decisively to outflank the enemy. In this battle, Alfonso of Castile captured the Prince of Morocco and a very impressive number of weapons, silver, and gold. He did not forget to show gratefulness for the prayers of Pope Benedict XII with lavish presents for the Pontiff.[42] Alfonso credited the resounding victory to the Virgin Mary's intercession. Accordingly, he ordered the construction of a magnificent sanctuary at Guadalupe in Extremadura. A grateful Alfonso of Portugal also commissioned a monument in front of the church of Our Lady of Oliveira, in Guimarães, Portugal.

Birth of a Race

The Reconquest of Spain was a titanic effort to expel the Muslim invader and recover the whole peninsula for Christ, but seven centuries of war had left the economy in shambles. On the positive side, Portugal and Spain produced some of their greatest men during that age, many saints, and great soldiers.

---

[42] Pope Benedict XII proclaimed the Papal Bull *Exultamus in Te*, declaring the war in Spain a Christian Crusade against Islam.

Those indomitable men would later cross the Americas on horseback conquering for the Spanish Crown a dominion that extended around the globe. They also gave the Church many new sons and daughters in Africa, the Antilles, Argentina, Bolivia, Brazil, California, Chile, Cuba, Paraguay, Peru, Colombia, Ecuador, Mexico, Texas, Venezuela, and the Philippines, taking the banner of the Christian Cross along with the Imperial flag. Those were the men that conquered the realm of Moctezuma and turned the pyramids of the ancient Aztec gods and demons into dust. Those forgotten men, born at the edge of the High Middle Ages, sailed across the globe to change the face of the world. They fearlessly fought in the service of Church and Crown. Saints they were not but their efforts made it possible for many nations, peoples, and tribes to know and worship the Savior of the world.

Ferdinand and Isabella

Ferdinand of Aragon and Isabella of Castile were cousins. They secretly married after receiving a Papal dispensation in October 1469, in Valladolid. The marriage united the crowns of the two kingdoms. To the west of Castile-Leon there was Portugal; to the east wedged between Aragon and Castile-Leon there was the tiny kingdom of Navarra; Aragon dominated the northern Mediterranean coast while the Muslim kingdom of Granada occupied the territory now known as Andalusia.

Ferdinand and Isabella are still known as the Catholic Monarchs of Spain. Both of them were devout followers of Our Lady of Guadalupe in Extremadura. They participated in the expansion of the Monastery. At that time, the town of Guadalupe and its monastic institution had grown in fame and extension. One of the most interesting items found in the Monastery is a very important codified collection of miracles. It is organized in nine codices containing about eighteen hundred documented miracles attributed to the intercession of Our Lady of Guadalupe.

The registry starts at the beginning of the 15th century and continues through the early 18th century. There are numerous miracles listed mostly about the liberation of Muslim captives, about help provided to the faithful when in danger or illness, and also many resurrections of infants similar to the resurrection of Gil Cordero's son.[43] It is important to remember this extraordinary list of miracles. When we delve deeper into the mysteries of Our Lady of Guadalupe both in her Spanish and Mexican advocations, we shall see a clear continuity. Meanwhile, we will return to our brief chronology of the Reconquest and consolidation of the Spanish nation.

---

[43] *La Fractura Historiográfica: Las Investigaciones de Edad Media y Renacimiento Desde el Tercer Milenio*; by Javier San José Lera, edited by Fco. Javier Burguillo and Laura Mier. Salamanca, Seminario de Estudios Medievales y Renacentistas, 2008.

During the reign of the Catholic Monarchs, three events of the utmost importance occurred: the territorial integration of the Spanish nation, the religious integration of Spain as a Roman Catholic country, and the conquest and evangelization of the Spanish dominions in New World. Spain was about to become a far-flung Empire in only one generation after fighting eight centuries to become a nation.

In 1482, King Ferdinand occupied Alhama and the War of Granada began. The campaign extended for ten long years finally ending in 1492 when Granada—the last Muslim bastion in the Peninsula"—fell under Christian control. The Monarchs returned to Extremadura to thank Our Lady of Guadalupe for the extraordinary graces received. They were also in search of peace and rest from the long and grueling war campaign. Following the conquest of Granada, Ferdinand and Isabella received Christopher Columbus in the royal monastery. There they signed the decrees funding the Genovese Admiral's expedition in search for a western way to the Indies.[44]

A New World for a New Nation

The discovery of a New World changed Spain forever. The Portuguese mariner Vasco da Gama had just managed to navigate the Cape of New Hope opening new routes of trade to India, China, and all the Orient. It took a while until the Spaniards realized that they had reached a whole new continent completely unknown to Europeans. In the years following Columbus' expeditions Spain, Portugal, and other European powers such as England, France, and Holland raced to grab as much territory as they could.

Spain quickly settled in what are now Santo Domingo, Cuba, Puerto Rico, and other islands. In 1519, Hernan Cortez arrived in Mexico, crossing from Cuba to the Yucatan Peninsula with about four hundred men, horses, and battle gear. The Spanish of that time wanted to evangelize the world. Their attitude would be incomprehensible for today's Christians—even for some Spaniards of our day. Their long ordeal resisting the Arian heresy in the early centuries, and the cruel Muslim invaders that remained in Spain for eight hundred years, grew in those men and women a strong sense of the Christian faith. Theirs was the first generation in centuries that could call themselves Spaniards. They were very proud of their great achievement: having forged a Christian country, under one crown and one flag against all odds. In the age of the German Reformation, they felt with good reason that they were commissioned to take the message of Christ to

---

[44] *El Norte de Africa en los Milagros de Guadalupe* by Gerardo Rodriguez; from *Estudios de Historia de España*; Volume XII, Tome 2, 2010.

the whole world. The old Roman spirit lived in them but their banners bore no longer the SPQR but the IHS.[45]

A Prayer to Save the Humble

When Cortez finally conquered Mexico, the Spanish soldiers wanted to reap the benefits of their long struggle. Many of them had left Spain knowing well that they would never come back. The economy in Spain was collapsed and many of those who volunteered to go to America were fleeing from a miserable and short existence as serfs in the motherland. They had braved the perilous passage across the Atlantic, they had survived a hostile reception, and they had won a war. Now Mexico was their only hope to realize their dreams of fame and fortune.

After Cortez was expelled from Tenochtitlan, he spent the best part of two years forging alliances with the enemies of the Aztecs. There were many that were against the whole business of being sacrificed on the altar of Huitzilopochtli. The discontented masses were ready for a leader, and Cortez was more than happy to oblige. The rulers of Tlaxcala were the first allies of Cortez. They converted to Christianity along with their families and subjects. After gathering a force about nine thousand strong, they felt capable of taking Tenochtitlan. The conquering of the Aztec Empire was not achieved by a powerful Spanish Army but by the alliance of a few hundred Spaniards with the natives of Cempoala, Tlaxcala, and Cholula. The rulers of the powerful Triple Alliance of Tenochtitlan, Texcoco, and Tlacopan were finally defeated on August 13, 1521.

During the war, a number of captured Spanish soldiers were sacrificed and eaten at the altars of Huitzilopochtli. Their comrades gathered on the lakeshore watched the horrible scene powerless to help them in any way. That had the effect of predisposing many Spaniards against the natives whom they considered a "creation of demons" and "no better than animals." The representatives of the Church did not agree with that conclusion and began the work of evangelizing the suffering people of Mexico against the will of some that wanted to enslave and exploit them. Violence erupted frequently and there were some cases in which even Catholic priests and other religious were violently attacked and killed by the dissident Spaniards who did not want the natives to be baptized. Those despicable men wanted to maintain the natives in ignorance of the Gospel and far from the Sacraments with a view to keeping them under their sway, exploiting them and killing them at will.

Informed of all that chaos, King Charles V named a new Bishop with extraordinary temporal powers to impose order in the land, and protect the natives from their rapacious Spanish overlords. The man selected for the task

---

[45] SPQR Latin for *Senatus Populus Que Romanus*, "The Senate and the People of Rome" and IHS Latin for *Iesu Hominum Salvator*, "Jesus Savior of Mankind."

was Don Juan de Zumarraga, a Franciscan of Basque origin. He arrived at a very difficult time when a general insurrection was taking place. There were groups of native converts who were persecuted both by rapacious Spaniards and by still unconverted natives. Some Spaniards followed the royal orders to protect the natives only to find themselves fighting other Spaniards. The result was a growing chaos that Bishop Zumarraga could not control. To make things worse, the rebels controlled all communications with Spain, making it impossible to report the grave situation to the capital. Finally, Zumarraga was able to smuggle a message to King Charles, letting the monarch know that "unless there is supernatural intervention" the country would certainly succumb to utter chaos.[46] After sending the grim news to the monarch on December 8, 1531, vespers of the Feast of the Immaculate Conception,[47] the poor Bishop prayed fervently for God's intervention, trusting himself to the intercession of the Mother of God.

---

[46] ".. si Dios no provee remedio de su mano, está la tierra a punto de perderse totalmente." *Raíces Marianas en Latinoamérica*, Universidad Católica de Loja, p. 166. 1ra Edición, 2012. Quoted in *María Devoción Popular*, by Eduardo Chávez Sánchez. Publ. by Librería San Pablo, Bogotá, Colombia.

[47] In 1531, the Catholic Church celebrated the Feast of the Immaculate Conception on December 9. That was later moved to December 8. The Oriental Churches still celebrate the feast on December 9.

4
THE CONVERSION OF MEXICO

We have seen how twelve years after the arrival of Hernan Cortez and about ten years after the end of the conquest of Mexico, the Church still struggled to Christianize the natives and keep order in the land.

With the arrival of Hernan Cortez, the natives of Mexico saw for the first time some signs of Christianity. Among them were several images of Our Lady of Guadalupe, the Patroness of Extremadura and Protector of Spain. The image of Our Lady of Guadalupe, so popular today, was still a decade in the future. Juan Diego was still Cuauhtlatoatzin, a commoner in his forties, living in the outskirts of Tenochtitlan. The Spaniards introduced the Spanish advocation of Our Lady in Mexico. The humble image was going to be once again the silent witness to the fall of a bloodthirsty oppressive empire. She had seen the fall of the Roman Empire; and the expulsion of the Muslim invaders from Spain. Now it was the turn of the Aztec Empire, the worshipers of the Left-Handed Hummingbird, the demon Huitzilopochtli.

Cortez learned very quickly that the Aztecs had set up a system of terror and oppression. About 25,000 men were required every year for the sacrifices performed by the temple priests. Of course, the subjects of Moctezuma did not like their oppressors and only needed a leader and a good opportunity to rise up in arms. The arrival of Cortez provided both a strong leader and the opportunity they had long hoped for. As soon as the Spaniards agreed with their new allies to fight against the Aztecs, the pagan temples were emptied of their idols and a copy of the image of Our Lady of Guadalupe was set in their place. When Cortez was finally received by Moctezuma and taken to the altars of their gods, the Spanish Commander astonished the king and his priests by destroying their idols. Cortez pushed their statues down the slopes still stained with the blood of recent sacrifices. After cleaning the altars, Cortez ordered his personal image of Our Lady of Guadalupe to be placed there along with a Crucifix.

In the days that followed, Cortez and his officers had to rescue that Crucifix and the image of Our Lady at great risk for themselves. That was the beginning of the war. The Aztec Empire fell only two years after the arrival of the Spanish conquerors. Theirs was the third pagan empire to fall before the humble image of Mary of Nazareth carved by Saint Luke. Some of the natives accepted the new faith patiently preached by Franciscans first, and later by the Augustinians. Juan Diego Cuauhtlatoatzin was one of the early converts. He was born in 1474 in the village of Cuautitlan. His native name was Cuauhtlatohuac, "he who speaks like the eagle." He was an artisan and merchant. Juan Diego was fifty-three, and already a widower when Our Lady of Guadalupe appeared to him on Tepeyac Hill.

At the time of the apparitions, Juan Diego lived with his uncle, Juan Bernardino in Tulpetlac, a village where there was no church. For that reason he had to attend Mass at Santa Cruz de Tlatelolco. He had lived most of his life under the Aztec rule; he was a young teenager when the Great Temple was built. It is possible that he was a witness of the thousands of human sacrifices offered that day. Juan Diego knew first hand the terror and oppression unleashed by the Aztecs on their humble subjects. Under Spanish rule, he was now under the oppression of cruel and immoral men. Juan Diego was a survivor of terrible times.

Only one day after Bishop Zumarraga poured his heart out in prayer for a supernatural solution to the growing chaos in Mexico, on Saturday, December 9, 1531, Juan Diego was on his way to hearing Mass. On the way to Tlatelolco passing by Tepeyac Hill, he heard birds singing so beautifully that he thought he was in Paradise. He stopped to enjoy the birds singing and when he looked up he saw a woman surrounded in radiant light. She was praying. As he went to greet her, she said that it was her wish that a temple would be built on that spot. She also commissioned Juan Diego to communicate that message to the Bishop.

Juan Diego obeyed and went to Tlatelolco. There he told the Bishop, who did not take Juan Diego seriously. A temple existed in Tepeyac dedicated to the Aztec goddess Toniatzin that was destroyed by the Spaniards during the war. Perhaps the simple man missed his ancient pagan goddess; perhaps he was imagining things. Bishop Juan de Zumarraga prudently told San Juan Diego to go back to that place and make sure his vision was a true one. Juan Diego returned to the hill and the Virgin Mary appeared to him there a second time. She told him to insist and go back to see Zumarraga one more time. Obediently, Juan Diego did as he was told but on this occasion, the Prelate instructed Juan Diego to ask the Virgin for a sign. Returning for a third time to the mountain, Juan Diego met the Virgin Mary again. Our Lady told him to come back the following day when she would give him a suitable sign.

Juan Diego's uncle, Juan Bernardino, fell seriously ill that Monday and poor Juan Diego had to care for him. Fearing the man was in danger of dying, he left him to seek the assistance of a priest who would give Juan Bernardino the last rites. It was Tuesday, December 12, quite early in the morning when passing by Tepeyac Hill he met the Lady from Heaven for the fourth time.

She inquired what was going on. He told her about Juan Bernardino's illness and the Lady informed him that his uncle was now in good health. Then she ordered him to climb to the top of the hill to pick some flowers. It was December, a time when frost ruins everything. We can interpret this strange request as a gentle test of Juan Diego's faith. Always docile with a childlike disposition, Juan Diego climbed to the top of the hill to find exquisite flowers in full bloom in spite of that being the coldest part of the hill and the most exposed to the chilling winter wind. He selected the most beautiful and filled his tilma with them, returning to the base of the mountain. Our Lady arranged the flowers in a motherly gesture of love and sent Juan Diego to the church in Tlatelolco, warning him not to show the flowers to anyone on the way but only to Bishop Zumarraga.

After arriving at the Bishop's residence, Juan Diego had to wait a while to be received. Servants tried to touch the flowers twice but both times the flowers miraculously disappeared into the tilma. Scared by the strange phenomenon, they hurried in and interrupted the Bishop who was at the time in the company of a group of people. Juan Diego then told the interpreter that he had in his ayate the sign that the Bishop had asked for. He then let the flowers cascade to the floor, revealing the humble cloth miraculously impressed "as if it was painted by angels"[48] with the image of Our Lady of Guadalupe. It was December 12, 1531, the year *metlactli omey acatl*, the 13th reed in the Aztec calendar. The 13th day that was made famous—386 years later—by the apparitions of Our Lady of Fatima in Portugal. The golden thread of Mary of Nazareth had touched the humblest of the humble in Mexico but that was only one more station in a long journey that started in the first century and would last many more centuries, all the way to our days.

The Virgin Mary appeared to Juan Diego at Tepeyac Hill in essentially the same way she had appeared to Gil Cordero in Extremadura many centuries before. We must consider the many similarities between both apparitions. The Mother of God introduced herself as Our Lady of Guadalupe to Juan Diego's uncle Juan Bernardino.

Many believe that the Spaniards heard "Guadalupe" when Juan Diego said "Coatlaxopeuh."[49] If that was true, the participants in the miraculous

---

[48] Was St Luke the painter of the tilma? The answer is perhaps reserved only to those blessed with a heavenly reward.

[49] "Coatlaxopeuh" means "She who crushes or dominates the snake" in the Nahuatl language. The author Gloria Evangelina Anzaldúa, an American scholar of Chicano cultural theory, feminist theory, and queer theory, favors "Coatlaxopeuh" as a possible American etymology for "Guadalupe" arguing— almost five centuries after the facts—that since the two words sound very similar, the Spanish heard "Coatlaxopeuh" as the equivalent of Guadalupe, as in Our Lady of Guadalupe, patroness of Extremadura. *Borderlands – La Frontera: The New Mestiza*, by Gloria Anzaldúa, 4th edition, p. 27.

apparition of Our Lady in Mexico had plenty of time to correct the mistake but they did not. The name Guadalupe remained because Our Lady wanted to give Mexicans the same dignity of the Spaniards who were already her children—in spite of the awful conduct of some individuals among them. Those revisionists who favor "Coatlaxopeuh" arguing from Indigenism do not realize that—used in that manner—"Coatlaxopeuh" is a divisive term, pitting native Mexicans against the European. The term "Guadalupe" achieves the opposite effect by uniting both races into a new one: under that name, both the Spanish from Extremadura and the Mexican Natives are now one; Mary of Guadalupe is telling them clearly: "You are brothers born of the same Mother."

As we have seen, that same Mother was present when the pagan Roman Empire, the Muslim Andalusia, and the Aztec Empire fell. We are beginning to see how throughout history Our Lady of Guadalupe destroyed the pagan gods, crushed the oppressors, and brought liberation to the oppressed.

Our Lady of Guadalupe arrived in Mexico in the same manner that she had arrived in Spain. Spain struggled to unite and become a nation; later Mexico was struggling not to collapse into utter chaos. In both cases, it appeared that the forces of evil had the upper hand. It seems that the Miracle of the Tilma was only the prelude of a greater miracle: the birth of a united Mexico as a new race, and a new nation. Nearly ten centuries were needed to forge the Spanish nation but Our Lady was about to give birth to modern Mexico in only a few days. The words of Isaiah 66:8 come to mind:

"Who has ever heard such a thing? And who has seen the like of it? Shall the Earth be brought forth in one day? Or shall a nation be brought forth at once, because Zion has been in labor, and has brought forth her children?"

Christendom had been born from the ashes of Rome, Spain had emerged from centuries of war and oppression, and now it was time for Mexico to be born, leaving behind a culture of death to bask in the glorious light of Christ the Lord of life.

Antonio Valeriano and the Nican Mopohua

All written narrations about the apparitions of Our Lady of Guadalupe are based on a document called the *Nican Mopohua*, written in Nahuatl using Roman characters at some time in the mid 16th century by a native Mexican scholar named Antonio Valeriano—one of the first to study in the Colegio de la Santa Cruz with Fr. Bernardino de Sahagún. The document was published by Luis Lasso de la Vega in 1649. Valeriano was a governor, a judge, and a scholar who mastered the Spanish language, Latin, and Classical Greek. He received the story related in the *Nican Mopohua* directly from Juan Diego Cuauhtlatoatzin. Antonio Valeriano wrote the *Nican Mopohua* to show clearly how the evangelization of Mexico progressed with the help of God and the Virgin Mary. In a very sober style, he states how the teachings of Christ reached the heart of both natives and foreign conquerors, and how they brought peace to people that could not be reconciled by any natural means. The story is developed as a series of concentric circles:

Heaven comes to rescue the Mexicans: The Virgin Mary appears to Juan Diego and asks for a church to be built on Tepeyac where Christ can be given to the people.

The Church is put on notice: News of the apparition reaches Bishop Zumarraga.

The religious fail to believe: The Bishop and his helpers fail to believe the humble messenger. In their distrust, they follow Juan Diego and he disappears before their eyes when crossing a causeway.

Three supernatural signs are given: fresh roses, a miraculous image appears on Juan Diego's tilma, and Juan Bernardino—uncle of Juan Diego—is healed and brought back from near death.

The conversion of Mexico: The city recognizes the message left on the tilma and surrenders to Our Lady's motherly love.

The Nican Mopohua

Here is told the orderly account of how the perfect Virgin Mary Mother of God Our Queen appeared recently at Tepeyac now renamed Guadalupe. She first appeared to a commoner named Juan Diego, and later her Precious Image appeared before the recently arrived Bishop Fray Don Juan de Zumarraga.[50]

It happened ten years after the conquest of the city of Mexico. When the weapons of war were deposed, there was peace in the towns around, and the faith began to flower in the knowledge of the True God for whom we all live.

Saturday, December 9. TheFirst Apparition

In the early days of the month[51] of December of 1531, there was a commoner, a native man called Juan Diego, a well-known neighbor born in Cuautitlan belonging to the parish of Tlatelolco. Very early on Saturday, he was on his way to church. The day was breaking as he passed near a hill called Tepeyac when he heard the singing of many precious birds. When the singing

---

[50] NOTE: The *Nican Mopohua* was written by Don Antonio Valeriano (1521–1605) in the Nahuatl language using Roman characters. He studied and later taught at the Franciscan Colegio de la Santa Cruz in Tlatelolco. Valeriano was fluent in Nahuatl, Spanish, Latin, and Greek having studied with Fray Bernardino de Sahagun, a renowned scholar of his time. I have translated a Spanish version of the venerable document, trying to render it in a way more easily readable in modern English, reducing some of the delightful flowery Nahuatl styles that sound a bit excessive in modern language.

[51] The Julian calendar day for December 9, 1531, was a Saturday. The Gregorian calendar was not implemented until October 1582.

of the birds paused then the mountain responded with a soft, delightful song. The song surpassed in beauty the singing of the bellbird of the marsh, the green parakeet, and other fine birds.

Juan Diego stopped and thought: Why am I deserving the grace to hear this? Am I dreaming? Maybe I am hallucinating? Where am I? What is this place? Maybe this is the place our forefathers talked about: the land of flowers, the land of plentiful corn, of fleshly pleasures, the garden of abundance, the heavenly realms perhaps?

He was looking over the hill towards the rising sun where that heavenly music was coming from. At one point, the singing ended abruptly and he heard someone calling from the hilltop: "Beloved Juan, beloved Juan Diego." He dared to move towards the call without a single concern in his heart, not feeling troubled in the least, feeling quite happy and content. He climbed the hillside following the voice that called him. Once he reached the top, he saw a young lady standing there who bid him come closer. When he approached, he marveled greatly at her perfect beauty and glory. Her garments glowed shining like the sun, and even the rocky crag under her feet glittered in the sunlight. Her brilliance surpassed that of the precious stones found in the most beautiful bracelets. The ground seemed to glow with the splendor of the rainbow in the mist. The mesquite and the nopal, the grass, the trees, and the bushes shone like emeralds; the foliage like fine turquoise; and the branches appeared bright like gold.

Juan Diego bowed before her and the Lady spoke: "Juan, my beloved, my little child, where are you going?" To which he replied: "My lady, my Queen, my beloved, I go to your holy house in Mexico, in Tlatelolco, to receive divine instruction from our priests, who are the image of Our Lord."

After that brief exchange, she revealed the purpose of her visit. The heavenly Lady said: "Be perfectly aware, my humblest son, that I am Holy Mary, the perfect ever Virgin Mother of the Truest God for Whom we live, the Creator of mankind, Master of the near and far, Lord of Heaven and Earth. It is my wish, my utmost desire that a holy house is built here for me where I will give Him to the people along with all my love, compassion, succor, and protection. I am truly your merciful mother, the mother of all the people of this land, and of all kinds of men who love me, who call for my help, seek me, and trust me. In that holy house, I will listen to their cries and sorrows, cure them of their many sufferings, miseries, and woes. To accomplish the wish of my merciful heart, go to the residence of the Bishop of Mexico and tell him that I am sending you to let him know how much I desire to have that house built for me, a temple here on the firm ground. You shall tell him what you have seen, revered, and heard. Be sure of my gratefulness and my reward. For this, I will give you riches and glory, and I will be rewarding you abundantly for your travails as you carry out this mission I am now giving you. You have heard the words I commanded you, my child, the humblest of my sons; go now and do your best."

Kneeling before her, Juan Diego answered: "My Lady, my beloved child, I am going to do your revered will as you so honorably commanded me. Now this commoner, the smallest and poorest of your servants will depart." Thus he departed immediately to do as instructed, taking the straightest way to Mexico.

Saturday, December 9. The First Meeting with Bishop Zumarraga

Once in the city, he went right away to the residence of the new Bishop, Don Juan de Zumarraga of the Franciscan Friars. There he begged servants to let the Bishop know he had an important message. They made him wait and eventually, the Bishop ordered him to come in. As he entered the Bishop's chambers, he knelt before the Prelate and told him everything about his mission—the gracious words of the Queen of Heaven, her message, and all the admirable things he had seen and heard. But the Prelate, having heard the whole story and her message, appeared not to believe it. His answer was: "My son, come again some other time and I will listen to you once again. Then I will consider from the beginning why you have come, your requests, and your intentions." After being dismissed, Juan Diego left, dejected because he could not accomplish his mission right away.

Saturday, December 9. Second Apparition

At dusk, Juan Diego reached the top of the hill. There he joyfully met the Queen of Heaven. She was waiting in the same place where he had seen her the first time. When he saw her he fell to his knees saying: "My Mistress, my Lady, my Queen, my Most Beloved Daughter, Smallest Child of Mine: I went as you commanded me to do your honorable will, your revered word. With difficulty, I reached the Bishop. I told him your command, your words, as you requested. He received me with all kindness and heard me attentively but from his answer, I gather that he did not understand me. He did not believe me. He said: 'My son, come again some other time and I will listen to you once again. Then I will evaluate and consider from the beginning why you have come, your requests, and your intentions.' By his answer, I realized he thinks that the house you wish to build here is but a product of my imagination, or perhaps that the request did not come from your lips. I beg you, my Lady, my Queen, my Beloved Child, so that your sweet words will be believed, to trust your message to someone nobler, someone of importance, well known, respected, and honored. I am truly a hired hand, a nobody, a pack animal, a tail, the end of the wing, a man of no importance. I cannot even carry myself but need to be led on by another man. You are sending me to unfamiliar grounds where I don't belong, my beloved Virgin, my Young Daughter, my Lady, the Smallest Child of mine. Forgive me, please for being the bearer of displeasure to your heart, for irritating you, and frustrating, my

Lady, my Owner." To that the perfect Virgin who is worthy of honor and veneration responded: "Listen to me, my son, the smallest of my children: be certain that I do not lack servants or messengers that can do my bidding, my word, my wishes but it is necessary that you do this personally. By your intercession, my will and my wishes will be accomplished. So I urge you, I insist, my youngest son that you go again tomorrow to see the Bishop. Make him understand on my behalf, let him hear my desire, my will to build the temple that I am asking for. Tell him again that I, the ever Virgin Holy Mary, the Mother of God, have sent you."

To that Juan Diego responded: "My Lady, my Queen, my Beloved: far from me to upset you. With pleasure, I shall go and do as you said. I will not fail to do it or consider the journey burdensome. I will do as you will although perhaps I won't be heard, and if heard, perhaps I may not be believed. Tomorrow at sunset, I will come to give you an account of the Bishop's answer. Now I take my leave and go rest for a while, my Daughter, my Small Child, my Lady, my Beloved." Then he went home to rest.

Sunday, December 10. Second Meeting with Bishop Zumarraga

Early on Sunday, Juan Diego left his house very early and went to Tlatelolco to get his religious instruction and be present for the roll call. Mid morning after Mass ended, he stood for roll call, and the crowd was dismissed. Then Juan Diego walked to the Bishop's residence and once again, with great difficulty, he was taken before his presence. He knelt before him and weeping he repeated the Virgin's message—sobbing, pleading, and hoping that the Bishop would believe it was the will of the perfect Virgin to build a house for her, a small sacred house in the spot she indicated. The Bishop questioned him about all details of the apparition and Juan Diego related everything without error. Even though he declared all things, and it appeared very clear that she was the perfect Virgin, the merciful, admirable Mother of Our Lord Jesus Christ, Juan Diego's words were not heeded.

The prelate told him that his petition could not be taken seriously on his word alone. A sign was necessary to prove that the Queen of Heaven sent him. On hearing the prelate's words, Juan Diego responded: "My Lord Bishop, please tell me what kind of sign you have in mind so I can ask the Queen of Heaven to provide it."

The Bishop verified all of his words and noticed that he did not doubt or hesitate, and then he dismissed Juan Diego. Once the poor man left, the Bishop ordered some trusted members of his household to follow Juan Diego and see where he was going, what company he kept, and whom he spoke with. They followed Juan Diego who was on his way along the main road. As he was crossing the bridge over the ravine near the Tepeyac causeway, the attendants completely lost sight of him. So they returned angry and frustrated to tell the Bishop the man had mysteriously disappeared. They convinced the

Prelate not to believe Juan Diego whom they deemed a liar and a dreamer. They were determined to punish Juan Diego harshly if he ever returned, charging him not to lie or disturb the people anymore.

Sunday, December 10. Third Apparition

Meanwhile, good Juan Diego was with the Most Holy Virgin, updating her on the Bishop's reply. After hearing him, the Lady dismissed him saying: "It is well, my son; you shall return here tomorrow to take to the Bishop the sign he has requested. With that sign he will believe you, he will not doubt your word or your intentions and know, my little son, that I shall reward you for all your travails on my behalf. Go for now; tomorrow I will be here waiting for you."

Monday, December 11. Juan Diego Cares for His Uncle

The next day, Juan Diego did not return. Arriving home that night, he found his uncle, Juan Bernardino, gravely ill. He summoned a doctor in the morning but there was no use, for Juan Bernardino was in grave condition. That night his uncle, feeling that his hour had come, asked Juan Diego to go early to Tlatelolco to find a priest to hear his confession and give him Last Rites because he was convinced he had little time left.

Tuesday, December 12. Fourth Apparition

Very early Tuesday morning, when it was still very dark, Juan Diego left for Tlatelolco to summon a priest. As he approached Tepeyac Hill, he hesitated. He turned west from the easterly road he was following, thinking: "If I go forward, I shall meet Our Lady, who will send me to give the Prelate the sign he asked for. First of all, I will take care of our troubles; I need to bring the priest, for my uncle is waiting and his hour is near." As he circled the hill, he crossed eastward towards Mexico to avoid meeting the Queen of Heaven and be delayed in his urgent errand. He imagined she—who can perfectly see everywhere—could not see him. Then he spotted Our Lady majestically descending down the hillside, for she had been watching him from the place where they met the previous day. She drew right near him and said, "What is happening, my son? Where are you going?" Maybe because he was embarrassed or ashamed, perhaps because he was afraid in her presence he replied: "My Young Lady, my Littlest Daughter, blessed are you. How are you this morning? Is your little body feeling well, my Lady, my Beloved? I am sorry to grieve you with bad news, to know that one of your poor servants, my uncle, is dying of a grievous illness that has overtaken him. I am hurrying on my way to Mexico to call a dear priest to hear my uncle's confession, for we mortals are born merely to wait for death. Once I have done this, I will return here to take your message. I beg your forgiveness, my Lady, my Beloved. Be patient with me, I am not deceiving you, I will hurry here tomorrow." After hearing Juan Diego, the perfect Virgin responded: "Listen, be assured in your heart, my youngest and dearest son, that this thing that disturbs you, this thing that afflicts you, is nothing. Do not let your countenance or your heart be disturbed. Do not fear this sickness of your uncle or any other sickness, nor any piercing or cutting thing. Am I not here? Am I not your Mother? Are you not under my shadow and protection? Am I not the source of your joy? Are you not in the hollow of my mantle, in the crossing of my arms? Do you need anything more? Let nothing else worry you or disturb you. Do not let this illness worry you because your uncle will not die now. Be assured that he is already well."

Later on, all learned that his uncle was cured at that very hour. When Juan heard those tender words from the Queen of Heaven, he was greatly relieved and his heart was at peace. Then he asked her to send him immediately to go and bring the Bishop the sign he had requested so that he too may believe. The Heavenly Queen addressed him again saying: "Climb to the hilltop, my youngest son, to the place where you saw me before. There you shall find plenty of flowers; pick them, gather a bunch, and come down at once to bring them here to me." Juan Diego went immediately.

When he reached the top, he was astonished to find a great variety of fine flowers blossoming out of season, for it was the cold part of the year. The flowers were fresh, diffusing their sweet perfume, still covered with dewdrops looking like precious pearls.

Juan Diego gathered the flowers in his tilma. The hilltop was a place where nothing ever grew except thorny bushes, prickly pears the natives call nopal, and mesquites in the midst of crags and rocks and if by chance there would grow some small weed, it was the month of December when the frost destroys everything.

Juan Diego went down the slope to bring the fresh cut flowers to the Heavenly Lady and when she saw them she took them delicately into her saintly hands. After arranging them she placed them in the fold of the ayate saying: "My youngest son, my little son, these flowers are the proof, the sign that you are going to bring to the Bishop on my behalf. Tell him to see in them my wishes and through them to accomplish my will. I place all my trust in you; you are my emissary. And I demand that you only open your cloak when you are alone in his presence to show the Bishop and only the Bishop what you are carrying. You will tell him everything, omitting nothing. You will tell him that I sent you to the top of the hill to cut the flowers, and then all the admirable things you saw. In such manner you will convince the Bishop to do his part and build the temple that I am asking for."

Having heard her commands, Juan Diego took off in joyful haste walking the road to Mexico, with the wonderful flowers he was carrying in his arms. Feeling no anxiety in his heart, and knowing that all was going to turn out well, he went on to complete his mission.

Tuesday, December 12. Third Meeting with Bishop Zumarraga

He took good care of the contents in the fold of his tilma, making sure that nothing was lost and enjoying the fragrance of the many precious flowers. When he arrived at the Bishop's residence, the servants came out to meet him. He pleaded with them to tell the Bishop how much he wanted to see him but none of them wanted to announce him. They feigned not to understand his words or perhaps they did not recognize him because it was still quite early and dark, or perhaps they recognized in him the importunate man that had been recently bothering them. It may have been also that they knew how he vanished in plain sight of his fellow servants when they tried to follow him. Juan Diego had to wait for quite a long time. When the servants saw how long he had been quietly standing there, and suspecting from his attitude that he was hiding something in the fold of his tilma, they approached him to find out what he was concealing. They would not stop bothering him, pushing, and even beating him.

Terrified that the flowers would fall to the ground, Juan Diego lifted a corner of his cloak to placate his tormentors. The flowers appeared fresh and fragrant to the gaze of the servants, and they marveled greatly because that was not the season for flowers to be in bloom.

They tried to take hold of them on three occasions but they failed because every time they tried to grab them, the flowers suddenly appeared as painted on the humble cloak. Astonished, they hurried to tell the Bishop about the strange phenomenon, and about how urgently the man had to see him, and how long he had been waiting, and so on. As soon as the Bishop heard this, he realized that the sign he was waiting for had arrived. He summoned the man to his presence immediately.

Juan Diego entered the room and knelt before the Prelate, telling him once again the marvels that he had seen: "Dear Bishop, I have done what you asked me to do. I told the Lady from Heaven, my Lady, my Heavenly beloved, Holy Mary, the Mother of God, that you have asked her for a sign so you could believe my message: that a little house is built in the place where she asked it to be erected. I also told her that I have promised you to come back with a sign, a proof of her will, just as you asked. She listened to your insistence, to your words, and she was pleased to receive your request for a sign so that her precious will might be accomplished. Early today when it was still dark she told me to come here to see you. I reminded her that she had promised to give me a sign that I could bring to you.

She immediately fulfilled her word. She sent me to the hilltop where I had seen her before, to cut various kinds of roses and once I cut them I presented a bunch to her. She took them in her holy hands and arranged them in the fold of my ayate so that I could bring them and give them to you in person. I knew very well that the top of the Tepeyac was not a place to find flowers in bloom since that is a place where nothing ever grows except thorny bushes, prickly pears, and mesquites in the midst of crags and rocks; I did not hesitate to go. When I climbed to the top of the hill I found a Paradise. There were all kinds of beautiful flowers, the finest flowers, covered with dewdrops, blooming splendidly, so I proceeded to cut a bunch. She instructed me to give you these flowers on her behalf so her precious will might be accomplished once you see the proof you have asked for. Now, believe the truth of my words. Here you have them, please accept them."

Then Juan Diego opened the fold of his tilma where the flowers were placed. As he allowed the beautiful flowers to cascade to the ground, they were changed into a sign: the beloved image of the Perfect Virgin Holy Mary, Mother of God, suddenly appeared in the same figure that we now behold in her precious little house, her holy little place in Tepeyac that is called Guadalupe. And when the Bishop and all who were there saw her, they fell to their knees and marveled greatly at her.

As they stood up to see her, they were saddened and with heavy hearts and somber thoughts. Even the Bishop wept in sorrow, pleading to be forgiven for not having obeyed her will before. Then the Bishop stood up and untied the tilma—where her image appeared as proof of her being the Queen of Heaven—from around Juan Diego's neck. Taking it, he placed it in his oratory and the Bishop received Juan Diego in his house as a guest for another day.

The Little House on Tepeyac Hill

The following day, the Bishop said: "Let us get up and go; show us the place where the Heavenly Queen wants us to build her a sacred house" and the people were urged to build it. Once Juan Diego showed them the place where the Heavenly Lady asked him to build a house, he asked permission to go home and see about his uncle Juan Bernardino, who was very ill when he had left him to call for a priest to hear his confession and assist him. The one that the Heavenly Queen said she had healed. The group would not let Juan Diego go by himself so they all went with him. When they arrived, they saw his uncle was healed and nothing at all afflicted him. In fact, it amazed his uncle very much to see his nephew being escorted and treated with great honor. So he asked Juan Diego why he was being treated with so much respect. Juan Diego told him that he had left him to summon a priest when the Queen of Heaven appeared to him at Tepeyac Hill and related to him how she had sent him to Mexico to see the Bishop so that he might build her a house in Tepeyac, and how Juan Diego was consoled when she told him not to be troubled, because his uncle was healthy.

His uncle confirmed those words and added that was the precise moment when she healed him. Juan Bernardino described her exactly as she had appeared to his nephew. She had told Juan Bernardino that she had sent Juan Diego to Mexico on an errand to see the Bishop. She also instructed him to inform Juan Diego of everything he had seen when he meets his nephew next time, including the marvelous way in which she had healed him, and that her beloved image should be named: "The Perfect Holy Virgin Mary of Guadalupe."

They brought Juan Bernardino before the Bishop so the Prelate could hear his testimony. The Bishop invited them to stay at his home in Mexico for a few days while the holy house of the Child Queen was being built at Tepeyac.

In time the Bishop moved the image of the Heavenly Maiden to the main church. He took her out of his oratory so everyone could see and admire her. The entire city—not one of them was missing—came to see it and marveled venerating her. They recognized her divine quality and offered their prayers to her, marveling greatly at how miraculously she had appeared among them, for absolutely no human hand had painted her beloved image.

Here ends the *Nican Mopohua* by Don Antonio Valeriano.

After the Miracle

The *Nican Motecpana*[52] is a document containing a whole lot of additional information about Juan Diego, his wife Maria Lucia, his uncle Juan Bernardino, and some additional miracles not mentioned in the *Nican Mopohua*. From the information contained in the *Nican Motecpana*, we can deduct that it took only thirteen days to build the first chapel at Tepeyac. The miraculous image was transferred from the Cathedral to its new home on December 26, 1531. Bishop Zumarraga, along with Juan Diego and Juan Bernardino, carried the precious tilma followed by all the Spanish authorities, the Aztec nobility, and every person in the surrounding area. It was a joyous occasion. Bowmen celebrated by shooting many arrows into the lake that surrounded most of the area at the time. One of those arrows accidentally hit a man in the neck, killing him instantly. The body of the poor man was taken before the image where the priests were proceeding. When the arrow was extracted from the victim, his wound healed immediately and he returned to life.[53]

The astonished crowd praised the Lady of Heaven, the perfect Saint Mary of Guadalupe. The first Christmas after the Miracle of Tepeyac marks the beginning of a period of conversions that would extend for a long time. Through those additional documents, we know that Juan Diego was a

---

[52] *Nican Motecpana* (Nahuatl, "here we present in orderly fashion") is a document similar to the *Nican Mopohua*, written in Nahuatl. The author is Fernando de Alva Ixtlilxochitl, writer, and historian of note who completed it in 1590, according to Don Carlos de Sigüenza y Góngora. The *Nican Motecpana* reports a chronology, men and women, and a series of miracles not mentioned in the *Nican Mopohua*. It is possible to cross reference many facts mentioned in the various documents: The *Annals of Puebla and Tlaxcala*, the Cathedral of Mexico general archives, the *Codex Escalada* and many others.

[53] This is one of the many parallelisms with the story of Gil Cordero of Extremadura whose dead son miraculously resurrected during his own funeral procession.

widower, his wife Maria Lucia had died two years before the apparitions, that he died in 1548 in a house built for him near the new chapel at Tepeyac. Bishop Zumarraga died that same year.

We also learn that Juan Bernardino died during the plague that affected the city in 1544, after having one last visit of Our Lady of Guadalupe who appeared near the day of his passing.

A Contemporary Controversy

Should we call her Our Lady of Coatlaxopeuh or Our Lady of Guadalupe? In my view, Our Lady was extremely clear. This apparition was not meant "for natives only" but also for the Spaniards causing trouble to Bishop Zumarraga, and also for those who would deny the natives their humanity and the grace of the Sacraments. In fact, Our Lady's message was meant to reach the whole world—something we will consider in depth later.

Our Lady of Guadalupe was very dear to the Spanish knights and the whole of Spain. The Mother of Extremadura and the Protectress of Spain was teaching the Spanish conquerors that she was also the Mother of the Mexican natives. Their two races had to become one race, one nation, under one Mother, one language, one King, and One God and Savior.

Juan Diego reports the name of Our Lady as "Guadalupe" and so does Juan Bernardino, and Antonio Valeriano and later on, multiple contemporary sources. Notice also that most of that business about changing the name of the advocation comes from revisionists, Marxists, Indigenists, etc. the usual crowd of dissidents but on the other side, we have various reliable written testimonies—two of them from the visionaries who saw and heard Our Lady face to face.

Those in favor of "Guadalupe" are in agreement with almost five centuries of the living tradition of the Church in this matter but the revisionists are telling us that it was all a misunderstanding, that Our Lady actually said, "Coatlaxopeuh"—meaning "She who crushes the snake" in Nahuatl. It is worth pointing out that the serpent is absent both in the vision of Juan Diego and also in the image of Our Lady of Guadalupe. Although the snake is present in many other images of the Virgin Mary, it is most conspicuously absent in the image given to the Mexicans. That should be sufficient to dismiss any argument in favor of "Coatlaxopeuh" as the original name.

Mary of Nazareth never instructed anyone to call her that way in Mexico. Coatlaxopeuh certainly is an attribute of our Lady when translated to our language and Christian imagery but Coatlaxopeuh was first an attribute of both Coatlique Toniatzin, the Mother Earth of the Aztecs, and also of the demon Huitzilopochtli the sworn enemy of Quetzalcoatl the feathered serpent. Imagine per absurdum if she had appeared to some other saint in Roman times saying: "I am Venus" because that name is connected in Latin to *venerari* ("to honor, to favor") and *venia* ("grace, favor")—Would that have been right? Those who espouse that view assume the Nahuatl translator and the Bishop were so simple and irresponsible as to supplant the allegedly given pagan name for one sounding more familiar to their ears.

The revisionists also argue that Juan Diego and Juan Bernardino could not pronounce Spanish sounds for the "g" or the "d" because they don't exist in Nahuatl—as if it was impossible for two grown men to learn new sounds! Consider Antonio Valeriano de Azcapotzalco who at one time spoke only Nahuatl: later he learned Spanish, Latin, and Greek! And then he studied Roman Jurisprudence and became a Judge for the Spanish Crown! So much for the so-called dumb Natives who allegedly were genetically incapable of learning two new sounds! That argument is so presumptuous it borders on racism! Consider also that Our Lady—who did all kinds of extraordinary things in that miraculous octave of the Immaculate Conception in 1531—could have easily taught them to retain and pronounce her name supernaturally. After all, it's just a "g" and a "d"—they did not have to learn theology or civil engineering!

Remember this was the same Mary that appeared in Fatima to three Portuguese children in 1917: Ten-year-old Lucia, nine-year-old Francisco, and seven-year-old Jacinta. Mary of Nazareth as Our Lady of Fatima trusted those small children with a message that the world had to obey to save the souls of billions. Does anyone believe that the children of Fatima could forget the message, perhaps because they were not used to dealing with the complex abstractions of history or theology? We are dealing with God's miracles here not with some forgetful human manager!

Mexicans to this day pronounce the Spanish "g" as an aspired "h" when followed by a diphthong (i.e. Sp. Guadalupe, agua, Paraguay) and so do most people in Central and South America. In fact, the same sound is present in the word "Nahuatl" or "Macehualtin"—Peninsular Spaniards have a more Germanic way of pronouncing the "g" however. So it was no big deal for Juan Diego to say "Huah-dah-loo-peh" using the aspired "h" he was more familiar with. That eliminates one of those "impossible to learn" sounds. Next is the "d" sound. In Spanish, the "d" sounds always like a soft "t", a sound pronounced by extending the tip of one's tongue a fraction of an inch forward under the upper front teeth. For someone who never had to soften a "t", it may be a difficult thing to do at first but not impossible.

I have observed that people lacking upper front teeth (a common thing in the Argentine countryside where I grew up) often pronounce the "t" noticeably softer. Even if Juan Diego mispronounced the name as "Huah-tah-loo-peh" it would have been close enough for any Spaniard to get it by approximation. That is why I believe the theory for calling our Lady using the Nahuatl word "Coatlaxopeuh" is so weak that it barely deserves serious consideration.

5

THE PARABLE OF TWO MEN

Spain began the exploration of the Americas at a time when the nation was beginning to consolidate as one political entity. That was the year when Columbus landed on the island of Santo Domingo. In that same year, King Ferdinand cleared the last bastion of Muslim occupation in Granada. Barely two decades later, Cortez began the conquest of Mexico. That amazing feat doubled the territory of the crowns of Castile and Aragon. The Spanish saying of that age was: "A Castilla y Aragón, Nuevo Mundo dio Colón."[54] The Spaniards were the first to call America "the New World." That is how the seemingly endless extensions of the new continent appeared to them.

The discovery of America contributed greatly in making Spain assume its new identity as a unified nation, turning the newly liberated country overnight into a worldwide Empire. The conquest of Mexico more than doubled the number of subjects living under the protection of the Spanish crown.

Not everyone was as happy as the lucky Spaniards of that generation. The end of the human sacrifices and the oppressive Aztec taxation was a blessing for the Mexicans but as soon as the unbearable Aztec system was gone, it was replaced by an almost equally unbearable rogue Spanish administration that began to despoil and exploit the native Mexicans in clear disobedience to the humane and just wishes of His Majesty Charles I.[55]

When Our Lady of Guadalupe appeared to Juan Diego, she effectively acted as a liberator for the Mexicans. Conversions multiplied and so did the mixed marriages; thus began the long process of integrating Mexico into one race and one nation. Our Lady of Guadalupe had been there when Spain was liberated from the Moors, and she was present in Mexico to liberate the natives from Aztec oppression first and from Spanish exploitation later.

The Miracle of Tepeyac divinely confirmed the native Mexicans as human

---

[54] "Columbus gave a New World to Castile and Aragon." Quoted from *Heráldica Hispalense* of October 11, 2013.
[55] Also known as Charles V, Holy Roman Emperor, he had inherited the kingdoms of Castile and Aragon from his mother, Juana daughter of Queen Isabella of Castile and King Ferdinand of Aragon.

sons and daughters of God. Once they were baptized, they could not be denied the grace of the Christian Sacraments; they were brothers in Christ just like any other European Christian. Our Lady of Guadalupe had miraculously given spiritual birth to a whole nation in a matter of days. When Bishop Zumarraga prayed for divine help to save Mexico on December 8, 1531—day of the Immaculate Conception—he had in mind a mere restoration of civil order and justice. The Holy Spirit heard his request and added to it by delivering much more. In time, civil order was restored, and soon millions of natives began to enter the Catholic Church to have their citizenship inscribed in the Divine Book of Life.[56]

Here we discover our first parallel: Spain—liberated from the Moors under the auspices of Our Lady of Guadalupe in Extremadura—came to America to liberate the Mexican people from Aztec oppression and made them subjects of the new Spanish Empire under the protection of Our Lady of Guadalupe in Tepeyac. In historical terms, two nations were born almost at once. The words of the prophet Isaiah could apply to the birth of both Spain and Mexico: "Who has ever heard such a thing? Who has seen the like of it? Shall the earth spring forth in one day? Or shall a nation be born at once, because Zion has been in labor, and has brought forth her children?"[57]

We can understand why Our Lady wanted to be known in Spain and Mexico as Our Lady of Guadalupe; she decided to be the Mother of both nations. Hernan Cortez and many of his companions were natives of Extremadura, where Our Lady of Guadalupe produced many admirable miracles resulting in the defeat the Moors. Portents like the Battle of Salado were not forgotten by the Spanish royal family, or by the commoners who fought under the banner of the Mother of God. Not bringing into this new realm the spiritual Mother of Spain would have been unthinkable for the Conquistadors.

Two Men of God

There are also many parallels between Gil Cordero and Juan Diego Cuauhtlatoatzin. Both were humble peasants, and pious family men who were suddenly in the center of supernatural events with important historical projections. Their encounters with Our Lady are similar in many ways. Our Lady of Guadalupe introduced herself to both men with like words, stating that she is the Ever Virgin Mother of God the Creator for Whom we all live, and the Redeemer of the human race.

Both men participated in revealing two different miraculous images of the Virgin Mary to the world. In both cases, a dear relative was supernaturally

---

[56] "For our citizenship is in Heaven; from where also we look for the Savior, the Lord Jesus Christ." Philippians 3:20.
[57] Isaiah 66:8.

made whole: one is the resurrected son of Gil Cordero, the other is Juan Diego's sickly uncle, Juan Bernardino.

Both Juan Diego and Gil Cordero were given a mission to convey divine orders to the Church and other authorities. They had to deal with incredulous people that were only convinced when a miracle happened before their very eyes.

Finally Juan Diego and Gil Cordero—each in his own country—were participants in the foundation of two national devotions to Our Lady of Guadalupe. Both of them were ordered to build a chapel and also were given the grace of consecration to Our Lady of Guadalupe by becoming the keepers of those sacred places.

Most importantly, Gil Cordero and Juan Diego are excellent examples of what a Catholic man should be. Their Marian devotion, their trust in God, their simple acceptance of the supernatural task entrusted to them, are all great virtues worthy of contemplation by every man who wants to serve God.

Gil Cordero and Juan Diego Cuauhtlatoatzin lived in different ages three centuries apart but both of them lived in times of turmoil. Their lives coincided with the "end of the world" in their own ages. Gil Cordero knew of the dangers of war that ended the Moors' occupation of Spain. He suffered the uncertainty of the hard times that followed once the long war was ended. Juan Diego lived most of his life under Aztec oppression and then lived through the collapse of the Aztec rule, and the emergence of the Spanish Colonial order. In his life, Juan Diego traveled in time from the Stone Age to the Modern Age, from the barbaric pagan institutions of ancient Central America to the Christian faith.

Gil Cordero and Juan Diego are spiritual models, each one a new Adam presented to the first generation of modern Spaniards and Mexicans. They are spiritual men gifted supernaturally with the ability to communicate a compact but very profound message. They are models of the men who will inherit the earth.[58] In the words of St Paul, the Apostle of Jesus Christ who lived also at the end of the ancient Jewish religious order: "The natural man does not receive the gifts of God's Spirit, for they are foolishness to him, and he cannot understand them because they are discerned spiritually. Those who are spiritual discern all things…"[59]

Humble men possessing the supernatural gift of understanding are essential for the salvation of their communities. God could not give the good news of peace to the likes of Moctezuma, or King Alfonso for they were natural men. The right disposition was found not among the greats of those nations but among the humblest: a Spanish cattle keeper, and a Mexican Macehualtin. Aristotle said that "the soul never thinks without images" and so

---

[58] See Matthew 5:1-11.
[59] 1 Corinthians 2:14-15.

God gave us two images through these two humble men.

Gil Cordero found the image of Our Lady of Guadalupe in Extremadura, Mary of Nazareth holding her son on her left arm, and a scepter in the right hand. The message, combined with the words of Our Lady, is very clear: "In time a great church, a noble house, and a great people will grow around this place." Spain as a Marian nation was going to be given the scepter, a kingdom, and the mission to take Christ to other nations, to be the mother of many new nations. Juan Diego was given a slightly different image of Mary, without a scepter, without a child in her arms but an image of a young girl surrounded by the sun's glory and pregnant. The very image of a new world filled with light and the promise of life, the very definition of what the Americas would be for so many generations of natives and immigrants. Gil Cordero and Juan Diego—through their humility, devotion, and obedience—are the men who make that bright future manifest to their people.

The Light of Humility, the Darkness of Pride

"Light shines in the darkness, and darkness does not overcome it. There was a man sent from God, whose name was John. He came as a witness to testify to the light so that all might believe through him. He himself was not the light, but he came to testify to the light. The true light, which enlightens everyone, was coming into the world."[60]

These words from the Gospel According to Saint John introduce us to the mission of John the Baptist who appears in history to prepare the people for the advent of Christ but they are also very fitting to describe the mission of these two most humble men—Gil Cordero and Juan Diego—who were also divinely selected to be precursors of Christ to their people at two different times in history.

The importance of these two men in history can hardly be denied. Juan Diego wondered why the Lady from Heaven would not choose someone more important, someone with a more respectable social or ecclesiastical status. In his humility, Juan Diego was puzzled by the ways of the Mother of God. The same happened to Gil Cordero who was a simple cattle herder. Both of them appeared before authorities suddenly expressing simple but perfect theological truths. We do not know for certain but it is quite likely that both men were completely illiterate. We can begin to understand the employment logic of Heaven when we consider the words of C. S. Lewis, the great apologist for the Christian faith: "Pride gets no pleasure out of having something, only out of having more of it than the next man ... It is the comparison that makes you proud: the pleasure of being above the rest. Once the element of competition is gone, pride is gone."[61] Pride was far from the

---

[60] John 1:5-9.
[61] *Mere Christianity*, C.S. Lewis.

hearts of Gil and Juan Diego. Both of them were well known for their honesty and humility. In the parable of the tax collector, Jesus reveals how God evaluates the hearts of men.

"He also told this parable to some who trusted in themselves that they were righteous and regarded others with contempt: 'Two men went up to the temple to pray, one a Pharisee and the other a tax-collector. The Pharisee, standing by himself, was praying thus, "God, I thank you that I am not like other people: thieves, rogues, adulterers, or even like this tax-collector. I fast twice a week; I give a tenth of all my income." But the tax-collector, standing far off, would not even look up to heaven, but was beating his breast and saying, "God, be merciful to me, a sinner!" I tell you, this man went down to his home justified rather than the other; for all who exalt themselves will be humbled, but all who humble themselves will be exalted.'"[62]

Regardless of their lack of education, wealth, or prestige, Gil and Juan Diego were spiritual men. The spiritual man is not self-centered; his concern is always how to be of service to others. On the other hand, pride is always self-concerned, self-oriented. Pride is an enemy of life, brings desolation to the soul, disturbs the heart, is a hindrance to consecration, and cannot lead to the knowledge of God.

What do John the Baptist, Gil Cordero, and Juan Diego Cuauhtlatoatzin have in common? All of them lived in times of crisis for their respective nations. Their mission was to announce great changes.

When the Virgin Mary revealed to Gil Cordero the location of her miraculous image, the poor cattle keeper could not possibly imagine that was the first step towards the total reconquest of Spain only three centuries later. The construction of a majestic monastery was still decades in the future, the expulsion of the Moors lays centuries ahead; the unification of all the Spanish kingdoms into one nation was unimaginable for the poor man! He had never been farther than a few miles from his hometown in his life. The existence, across the ocean, of a shining New World full of riches and the imperial destiny of Spain, would have appeared to him as a chimera. Yet all of that utter ignorance only enhances the value of his profound faith. The same can be said of Juan Diego who chose to perform the humblest duties in that first chapel on the Tepeyac—after being the center of the most extraordinary event ever to happen in the Americas!

We know through Jesus that John the Baptist was an extraordinary person, the most important prophet ever; bigger than Moses, and Elijah, and all the other prophets: "In truth I tell you, among those born of women none has risen greater than John the Baptist, yet whoever is least in the Kingdom of Heaven is greater than he."[63] Well, John the Baptist was great but not proud,

---

[62] Luke 18:9-14
[63] Matthew 11:11.

he was one of the humblest men to walk the earth. We know he was humble because he was not at all concerned about himself: he ate locusts and wild honey, and was not what we would call today "a slave to fashion." His focus was on announcing the Messiah and a new age of glory for the people of God. His ministry called people to humble repentance, to a life of modesty, and a return to the Law of God. John the Baptist was not a proud man at all.

The proud man is always self-centered to a degree but true humility requires paying attention to others. If we observe carefully, we can see that "focusing on others" came naturally to John the Baptist, Gil Cordero, and Juan Diego. They were important people but their importance was a consequence of their humility. Who can be more important than someone heavenly selected for a mission?

That absence of pride, that profound humility present in John, Gil, and Juan Diego is there for a reason: they are each one the archetypes of the Jew, the Spaniard, the Mexican. Our Lady of Guadalupe teaches that through her image. She is the model of humility and modesty, she is a Jewess, and a Queen but she chose to be represented as a maiden princess of mixed race, a Mestiza. From that humble position, she introduces us to our mission of ridding the nations of their oppressors, their demonic overlords. She was present when the pagan gods of the Greco-Roman world fell before Christ. She was also present during the long push to expel the Mohammedans from Spain. We have seen how she was also present when Cortez reduced the demonic temples of Mexico to rubble.

Real Men Are Needed

Gil and Juan Diego were also real men, family men, husbands, and fathers. They are lacking the self-centered quality of pride but they are perfectly self-aware in their humility. They accept the mission given to them knowing that it will be difficult, even humiliating. I can imagine the sarcastic thoughts of their contemporaries: "So, the Virgin Mary, the Queen of Heaven came to this unlikely place and she chose to communicate with someone who was herding cattle? Sure ... that is what Queens do all the time!" We also read in the *Nican Mopohua* how poor Juan Diego was subject to all kinds of humiliations, including waiting for hours without heat, without a meal, and wearing clothes inadequate for that time of the year. Imagine walking ten miles through the Mexican countryside in December, on sandals with a humble ayate for cover. Now imagine walking that distance back and forth four consecutive days, knowing very well that rejection awaits you. Yet Juan Diego persevered with manly perseverance, and when he was finally proved right he offered himself to sweep the floor in the new chapel. "Truly one day in your temple courts is better than a thousand elsewhere. I have chosen to be a doorkeeper in the house of my God, rather than to dwell in the tents of the wicked."[64]

Consecration comes naturally to Gil Cordero and Juan Diego. They both chose to live the rest of their lives as simple keepers of a lowly chapel as long as they can be counted among the family of the Virgin Mary, just like John the Baptist. Their sacrifice is not small but it produces results. Gil Cordero and Juan Diego are spiritual fathers, chosen by Our Lady of Guadalupe to spiritually inseminate their nation, their land with the seed of Christ. We know that from the words of Mary to Juan Diego: "I want a house built here, where I can give you my Son." She prophesied to Gil Cordero in a similar fashion: "In time a great church, a noble house, and a great people will grow around this place." The two visionaries were spiritual pioneers chosen to spearhead Christ's conquest of their lands.

Moctezuma was the Emperor of Mexico, the inheritor of the throne of Tlecaellel, the ruler of the Triple Alliance, the proud Ruler of the Realm of Huitzilopochtli but all those titles only delivered death to Moctezuma's kingdom. Pride always results in death. Picture the pride in the heart of the Aztec kings and priests who believed their sacrifices were essential to bring the sunrise every morning. Their mythology talked about sustaining life while the dead piled by the tens of thousands year after year.

John the Baptist condemned a legalistic religious system that was spiritually dead. Gil Cordero had his vision of the Virgin Mary at a time when a sizable portion of Spain lingered under Muslim rule. Juan Diego was instrumental in the conversion of millions of Mexicans who were captive to diabolical games of murder and tyranny. Those men opened the doors to Christ to revive the nation. In the mysterious order of Heaven, life and healing come through the smallest of all servants. To reorder the Jewish world, God sends a young maid, Mary of Nazareth. Mary is at the center of the renewal of Israel who finds its universal mission in the Church. She also appears in Spain at Guadalupe in Extremadura to begin to make a world power out of a former Roman province occupied by Muslim barbarians. Finally, she appears in Mexico at Tepeyac to liberate millions of Mexicans from superstition and despotism.

In my mind, the lives of Gil Cordero and Juan Diego are a living parable calling Catholic men to imitate their virtues. First, humility in service: to focus on serving God through serving our neighbor. Second, to spiritually inseminate the culture with the Gospel of Jesus Christ, effectively reflecting the paternity of God. Third, to consecrate one's life to Christ through Mary Most Holy, serving the Church, and advancing the cause of life. That is the ultimate destiny of Europe, represented in this parable by Spain that contains almost all the races of the European continent. It is also the ultimate destiny of America, represented in our parable by colonial Mexico, the country that occupies the center of the American continent and has become also a crucible of races.

---

[64] Psalm 84:1.

The challenge to the Church today is not bigger than those King Charles I of Spain or Bishop Zumarraga had to face. The solution to our crisis is still the same: falling to our knees in faithful prayer just like that poor beleaguered Bishop did when faced with a dead end. Gil Cordero also prayed fervently for the resurrection of his young son in spite of the rejection and disbelief he had to live through.

Christ sent us those men because undoubtedly he loved those nations. When we are lost he draws near, he takes care of our needs. We love him also but somehow we manage to place obstacles between him and us. Our own imperfections keep impeding a full union with Christ. We tend to complicate the matter; we lack the simplicity and the strength of Gil and Juan Diego. But this problem remains: our disordered affections make our full union with Christ quite difficult. The nations of the world today need Christ but lack men with the virtues of Gil and Juan Diego. Our societies are afflicted by many maladies. But lost in our pride, we fail to see that we are not going to succeed without Christ: "I am the vine, you are the branches. Those who remain in me and I in them bear much fruit, because separated from me you can do nothing."

Gil Cordero and Juan Diego Cuauhtlatoatzin are still perfect models of how to deal with hard times, how to live before God, how to save the world one soul at a time. Their smallness was what God used to accomplish easily what the great men of our age cannot fathom.

6

THE VISION

We have briefly reviewed the history of the two nations visited by Our Lady of Guadalupe in her two apparitions, one Spanish and one Mexican. We have also examined the lives of the two visionaries, Gil Cordero and Juan Diego Cuauhtlatoatzin. We have followed the miraculous image of Mary of Nazareth from the days of St Luke the Evangelist, to the Reconquest of Spain, the discovery of America, the Conquest of Mexico by the Spaniards, and the supernatural impression left by the Queen of Heaven on the tilma that once clothed a simple Macehualtin, Juan Diego. We have learned about the pure masculinity of both visionaries forever tied to the birth of their nations, and the history of salvation. The vision of Tepeyac is not the end of that wonderful voyage. When Juan Diego met the Mother of God, he was given first an auditory treat, the song of birds, a sweet sound designed to prepare him for the vision ahead of him. Mothers sometimes sing to make their children sleep, Mary is no different. In reality, she is more of a mother to us than our own mothers could ever be because she is the archetype of motherhood and those born of her will live forever. That morning of December 9, 1531, she arranged the song of birds to alert Juan Diego to the realities of Heaven that she was about to show him. That pure music, coming from God's living creation, was accompanied by the song of the very hill where Juan Diego was standing. Adam was alerted by the voice of God in the Garden of Eden (Genesis 3:10) and the Roman faithful processing with the image of Our Lady heard angels singing as they passed Castel Sant'Angelo.

I wonder if there is a connection between that brief morning concert and the natural talent for song and music that nearly all Mexicans have. Music has the power to affect our thoughts and our mood. Scientists have found recently that music can positively affect the development of intelligence in children, even in the womb. That song was very different from the religious music that Juan Diego could remember from infancy, the frantic beat of the demonic snakeskin drums, sounding at the hour when human sacrifices were offered.

He stopped to look but he did not trust his own senses. "I must be dreaming," he thought. The experience was intense enough for him to dismiss that first idea. "Perhaps I am in Paradise," the land of eternal spring, of flowers and abundance, the netherworld described in the Aztec religion. His pagan ancestors believed in nine underworlds, represented by each moon in the human period of gestation, but Juan Diego's instincts were already guided by his incipient Christian formation. Instead of looking around to ascertain his whereabouts, something made him look up to the top of the hill. The Tepeyac, like a precious jewel, basked in the glory of the rising sun. Now all of Juan Diego's senses were focused and ready. This was not an ordinary sunrise.[65]

Suddenly the birds stopped singing. There was a brief silence and then he heard the sound of his own Christian name pronounced by the sweetest voice: "Juan Diegotzin."

It is very difficult to explain the use of the diminutive in the Nahuatl language. Even to this day, Mexicans use the diminutive to express affection in Spanish. Lovers call their beloved "mi pequeñita" (my little one) and even Our Lady of Guadalupe is well known as "La Morenita" never disrespectfully but with profound affection. In Nahuatl however, the diminutive carries a meaning similar to the royal treatment in other languages. I found one close example in the well-known English anthem:

God save our gracious Queen!
Long live our noble Queen!

If *per impossibile* someone had to sing that in Nahuatl, the word "Queen" would be in the diminutive-honorific as a moving expression of faith, exultation, and profound respect: gracious, noble, and beloved would be expressed by the addition of the syllable "tzin". The sweet voice calling Juan Diego was using that form. Our humble Macehualtin was treated with honor and love from the start.

We know our Saint did not fret like others who had encountered heavenly visitors. Observe that nearly everyone experiencing the numinous, even great saints, tend to feel afraid. The Prophet Ezekiel fell with his face to the ground when he had his vision of the chariot of God[66] but something in the voice of the person calling gave him the strength necessary to stand in a dignified manner before the Throne of God: "He said to me, 'Son of man, stand on your feet, and I will speak

---

[65] In fact, there were only four days left to the Solstice of Winter which the Aztecs considered the birth or renewal of the Sun. That year marked the beginning of the Age of the Fifth Sun in the Aztec Calendar. The European Julian Calendar was lagging about nine days by 1531. Spain would not adopt the more precise Gregorian Calendar until fifty years later.

[66] Ezekiel 1:1-28.

with you.'" When He spoke, the Spirit came into me and made me stand on my feet."[67]

In contrast with Ezekiel, the children involved in other apparitions of Our Lady were not afraid. Innocence is not scared when experiencing a heavenly vision. What the *Nican Mopohua* tells us about Juan Diego's disposition is a good indication that his heart was as pure at that of a child but he had also a brave, masculine heart devoid of the fear of death.

Confidently, Juan Diego advanced towards the voice and "his heart was not disturbed and he felt extremely happy and contented" as he climbed the hill. Juan Diego was a 54-year-old man at the time of the apparitions; he was likely to be a seasoned fighter trained from youth to survive the Aztec flower wars if needed. He knew very well that those standing on a hill have the advantage over those climbing, and yet he climbed confidently with a trusting heart. That confidence was instilled by the celestial voice calling him with the same power that gave the Prophet Ezekiel the strength to stand up before God's chariot.

After ascending a distance towards the voice, he saw a young maiden bidding him come closer. This is another indication of Juan Diego's purity of heart. I am quite sure that impure eyes were never allowed to look upon Our Blessed Mother. Perhaps our saint was prepared for this encounter by many years of ascetic life and contemplation of the newly learned Christian mysteries. He was privileged to see the glorified presence of the Virgin Mary, something only a few saints had seen before. His reaction was one of saintly admiration.

The Maiden from Heaven was shining as if she was dressed in waves of light. Her glorious presence seemed to transform the landscape surrounding her. Seeing that, Juan Diego knew that she was sanctifying the Tepeyac even before she uttered a single word about building a church there. When Joshua met the Angel of Israel[68] he was told: "the place where you stand is holy ground" because the presence of the Angel had a purifying effect on the land. The Perfect Virgin Mary, as the Spouse of the Holy Spirit, blessed with her presence the ground of the Cerrito in the same manner described in the Golden Sequence for the Mass for Pentecost:

---

[67] Ezekiel 2:1-2.

[68] Once when Joshua was near Jericho, he looked up and saw a man standing before him with a drawn sword in his hand. Joshua went to him and asked him, "Are with us or against us?" The man replied, "Neither; but as commander of the army of the LORD I have now come." And Joshua fell on his face to the earth and worshiped, and he said to him, "What do you command your servant, my lord?" The commander of the army of the LORD said to Joshua: "Remove the sandals from your feet, for the place where you stand is holy." And Joshua did as he was told. (Joshua 5: 13-15)

Veni, Sancte Spiritus,
et emitte caelitus
lucis tuae radium [...]
Lava quod est sordidum,
riga quod est aridum,
sana quod est saucium.[69]

Juan Diego saw the crags about him transformed, beaming light like precious stones, reminding us of the vision of the New Jerusalem seen by St John:

"The wall was made of jasper, and the city of pure gold, pure as glass. The foundations of the city walls were adorned with every precious stone: the first was jasper, the second sapphire, the third agate, the fourth emerald, the fifth onyx, the sixth ruby, the seventh chrysolite, the eighth beryl, the ninth topaz, the tenth turquoise, the eleventh jacinth, and the twelfth amethyst. The twelve gates were twelve pearls, each gate made of a single pearl. The great street of the city was made of gold, pure and clear as glass."[70]

Even the prickly nopal cacti appeared to Juan Diego as made of emeralds. For the Mexicans of that age, few things were more precious than emeralds and jade. In this part of the vision, the thorns of the nopal were transformed into something most desirable. That image is a figure of the glory of Heaven awaiting the faithful after the sufferings of the Cross.

"The earth seemed to shine with the brilliance of a rainbow in the mist" the same rainbow that sealed the promises of a new world in times of Noah, the rainbow that the Aztecs painted on the vestments of their god of rain, Tlaloc. Now the vision, the image completes the Aztec idea of divine blessings, conveying the idea of mother earth (Coatlicue Toniatzin,) the life-giving sun rays (Tonatiuh,) and the gentle rain (Tlaloc) blessing the land with the promise of a good harvest. Ascending majestically towards the knowledge of Heaven is "the one that speaks like an eagle," the Cuauhtlatoatzin aptly representing Cuauhxicalli, the sacred eagle-vessel. The meaning of this part of the vision is in my mind, very obvious: Heaven is putting together a parable using the symbols familiar to the Mexican people. The gentle teaching of Heaven is clear: Juan Diego is the chosen vessel[71] who will be elevated to

---

[69] Come, Holy Spirit, / and from Heaven send /the radiant light of your beams [...] / Wash away our impurities, / water our barren soil, / and heal our wounds.

[70] Revelation 21:18-21.

[71] For a better understanding of the image, consider Acts 9:15 – "But the Lord said to [Ananias], 'Go, for he [Saul of Tarsus] is an instrument whom I have chosen to bring my name before Gentiles and kings and before the people of Israel." See also Acts 9: 1-19 where God prepares Saul of Tarsus through a vision to become Paul, the Apostle to the Gentiles. God also prepares Juan Diego in a similar manner to take the Gospel to the Mexicans. However, the gentle disposition of the Mexican contrasts with Saul of Tarsus' ardent persecution of the flock of Christ.

Heaven carrying not a bleeding heart of flesh but the purity of his own heart as a sacrifice acceptable to the true God. So through this selected vessel Cuauhtlatoatzin, a heart purified by so many sufferings, God will be finally revealed to the Mexican people after centuries of darkness.

> *O Lord, open my lips,*
> *and my mouth will declare your praise.*
> *For you have no delight in sacrifice;*
> *if I were to give a burnt-offering, you would not be pleased.*
> *My sacrifice, O God, is a broken spirit;*
> *a broken and contrite heart, O God, you will not despise.*[72]

The mission of the Talking Eagle begins at this encounter at Tepeyac. What follows is a marvelous lesson that will be condensed in his vision, and impressed upon his humble tilma.

> *God gives power to the faint,*
> *and strengthens the powerless.*
> *Even youths will faint and be weary,*
> *and the young will fall exhausted;*
> *but those who wait for the Lord shall renew their strength,*
> *they shall mount up with wings like eagles,*
> *they shall run and not be weary,*
> *they shall walk and not faint.*[73]

Juan Diego the talking Eagle will gladly walk many miles in the days following his first vision. The effort that would tire even a young man will not tire his five-decade-old body. He will be charged with taking his nation to God, and God Himself is infusing him with the strength to deliver the Divine Gospel.

The *Nican Mopohua* continues: "He prostrated himself in her presence, listening to her voice and to her words, which were full of praise, very affable, as those of someone who wished to attract him and esteemed him highly."[74]

Juan Diego's heart is in the right place. He did not have to be knocked off his feet like Saul of Tarsus. He understood who was addressing him. Prostration was the proper attitude along with paying careful attention to the words of the Lady from Heaven.

---

[72] Psalm 51: 16-18.

[73] Isaiah 40: 29-31.

[74] Quoted from *Our Lady of Guadalupe* by Lawrence Feingold, from *Three talks given at the Rigali Center*, May 5-7, 2009, transcription published by Ave Maria University, Institute for Pastoral Theology.

We know that Juan Diego understood he was seeing the Perfect Virgin Mary by the manner he answered the Lady's question: "Quimolhuili – 'Tlaxiccaqui noxocoyouh Juantzin, campa in timohuica?'" That is: "She said unto him, 'Hear, my beloved, my youngest son, Juantzin: where are you going?"

To which Juan Diego respectfully answers, revealing his understanding that The Lady is the Celestial Queen of the Church: "My Lady, my Queen, my Beloved Maiden! I am going as far as your noble little house in Mexico-Tlatelolco, to pursue the knowledge of God there taught to us by those who are the image of Our Lord, our priests."

Then the Lady of Heaven does the following:

She confirms her identity.

She states her desire to build a "little house" for her at the Cerrito.

She states her purpose, to give her Son to the people.

She orders Juan Diego to inform the Bishop of Mexico.

Juan Diego greets her most respectfully and departs "immediately to do as instructed, taking the straightest way to Mexico."

The Eagle Struggles Heavenward

Bishop Zumarraga had recently arrived with both ecclesiastical and temporal powers to take care of the dangerous situation developing in Mexico. A number of Spanish authorities were dispossessing the Mexicans, exploiting them, and in many cases murdering them mercilessly. Cortez was away in Spain standing trial at the Royal Court because of false accusations, and trying to save his reputation as a loyal servant of King Charles. The Mexican converts were under constant pressure from those who wanted to return to Aztec rule, in addition to being attacked by avaricious Spaniards coveting their land and possessions. The natives vastly outnumbered the Spaniards, and they were beginning to rebel in some areas. The country was a tinderbox waiting for a spark to ignite a general rebellion. Some of the Spaniards loyal to the Crown were trying to inform the King but the rebels were in control of all communications with the Royal Court.

A serious insurgency menaced the Mexican domain of King Charles V. Bishop Zumarraga was a man of strong faith and he did what a man of faith does when facing a desperate situation: he fell to his knees and poured prayer after prayer before the Lord. The day of the Immaculata, December 8, 1531, in a secret report sent to King Charles, he briefly wrote: "Unless there is supernatural intervention, the country is lost." After that, he trusted the country's troubles to the Immaculata and went to sleep.

The answer to his prayers did not tarry long. While he was still asleep, the morning of December 9, Our Lady of Guadalupe was appearing to Juan Diego Cuauhtlatoatzin, the one that speaks like an eagle. By the time Bishop Zumarraga kneeled to pray the first prayers of the Daily Office, Juan Diego was hurrying towards the Bishop's residence with a message from the Queen of Heaven herself.

When Juan Diego arrived at the Bishop's residence, he waited patiently, bearing the morning cold until he was allowed to see the Bishop. We can imagine the scene; the Bishop was well guarded, due to the perilous situation developing outside the walls of his palace. That may be the reason Juan Diego was made to wait a prudential time. But there was another reason. In spite of his conversion and exemplary life, he was a despised Macehualtin, barely a man in the eyes of the Aztec society. When it became evident that Juan Diego was not dangerous, the guards most likely took him for a lunatic. But Bishop Zumarraga was a real man of God—we have to thank God for the Franciscan order—what would have been of Mexico if it was not for the good heart of Don Juan de Zumarraga. The King had met him years ago while Don Zumarraga was preaching a retreat for the men of the Royal House. Charles V was also a man of God, profoundly Catholic for a prince of that era; he was the son of Phillip the Handsome, and Joan of Castile. Through his mother, he was the grandson of Queen Isabella of Castile, and King Ferdinand of Aragon. He was arguably one of the most Catholic men ever to sit on a royal throne. When news of injustice and exploitation of his Mexican subjects reached him, he quickly invested Don Juan de Zumarraga with the title of Bishop and the powers of a temporal Viceroy.

The morning of December 9, 1531, when Juan Diego the beloved Eagle informed Don Juan of his earlier encounter with the Virgin Mary, surely the good Bishop remembered his prayers begging God for help. Through a translator, he heard the report of Juan Diego, sending him off with a promise to think about it and hear the report again some other time.

Juan Diego departed, sadly convinced that his low station in life was the cause why the Bishop would not believe his report. He walked back to the Cerrito with a heavy heart. Our Lady was waiting for him at the same place. Prostrating before her, Juan Diego told her the sad news. The Bishop was not inclined to believe a poor Macehualtin, a commoner of no importance like him. Juan Diego begged Our Lady of Guadalupe to take into account how small and how utterly unimportant he was.

Failure and mercy

What is not very apparent here is that Juan Diego is begging for his life because his mind was still influenced by his Aztec upbringing. He had been given an errand by the Christian equivalent of Coatlicue Toniatzin, in the very hill where the old temple of the goddess used to stand. Remember that Coatlicue gave birth to her children and also took their life without remorse. In his mind, Juan Diego was a total failure and thus he expected to be punished for his faults. The Aztec gods were not merciful at all, as it befits monsters thirsty for human blood and flesh. Juan Diego was expecting the old obsidian knife to tear into his chest; he felt he had to satisfy Our Blessed Mother for his shameful failure to convey a simple message.

His discourse is the plea of a man whose heart was broken by years of demonic pressure placed upon him by a barbaric and uncompassionate religion, by a brutal taxation system that left his tribe with no room for error, always working to survive one more unmerciful year. This was a man who lived all his life watching his peers dismembered by the Aztec priests after working a lifetime like beasts of burden to fulfill the demands of the tax collectors.

Here is where the tender care of the Mother of God comes to console Juan Diego. With affectionate words, she explains that he is the one chosen to be her ambassador, the messenger. Hinting at the future elevation of Juan Diego to sainthood, she calls him an intercessor of Heaven:

"Listen to me, my son, the smallest of my children: be certain that I do not lack servants or messengers that can do my bid, my word, my wishes but it is necessary that you do this personally. By your intercession, my will and my wishes will be accomplished. So I urge you, I insist, my youngest son that you go again tomorrow to see the Bishop. Make him understand on my behalf, let him hear my desire, my will to build the temple that I am asking for. Tell him again that I, the ever Virgin Holy Mary, the Mother of God, have sent you."

Imagine the relief of our poor Juan Diego! He was not going to be hit by a bolt from above; his chest was not going to be opened by the priestly knife. This was not Coatlicue Toniatzin, the one dressed in a skirt made of snakes, the maker, and killer of her own children. He had met her at sunrise, and the again at dusk at "the hour when the sun dies", and yet he was still alive. Even after failing he still had a mission, and more than a mission: a destiny.

The second sunrise

The next day, Juan Diego got up early again to walk the usual thirteen miles to Tlatelolco. After attending Mass and receiving his religious instruction he directed his steps to the Bishop's house. He was ignored by the servants again and had to wait a long time to be received. Once before the venerable Bishop, Juan Diego begged him with tears to believe the word of the Virgin Mary. This time the Bishop asked him many questions to ascertain the veracity of the message and the integrity of the messenger. Something was beginning to break the Bishops skepticism. First of all, he had reports that Juan Diego was a good man that had a saintly reputation. The message delivered by the poor native was theologically correct, even when pressed for information, Juan Diego was consistent and sincere. What was going on? Obviously, a barely formed catechumen from a culture so foreign to Christian Spain could not possibly make up such a theologically perfect scam. Was one of the local Catholic priests involved? Zumarraga knew that some of his priests were sympathetic to the heretical teachings of a German monk, Martin Luther, who was causing quite a lot of trouble in Germany. Was someone trying to fusion the old cult of Coatlicue Toniatzin with Christianity to gain the loyalty of the poor natives and start a rebellion? Was this a trick of the devil seeking to reinstate the old demonic religion of the Aztec Empire? Or was this man the answer to his fervent prayers for a supernatural intervention to save the Dominion of New Spain, and the King's Mexican subjects?

Just in case he instructed Juan Diego to bring back some proof of his contact with the Virgin Mary. The native agreed and left not without promising the Bishop that he was going to ask Our Lady of Guadalupe for proof of her visitation.

The Bishop had enough trouble in his hands but he decided to investigate the strange incident discreetly by sending two men to spy on Juan Diego but the men lost track of him in the middle of the causeway, the man miraculously vanished before their very eyes. That report must have intrigued the Bishop even more.

A short time later Juan Diego was once again at the Cerrito, reporting to the Lady of Heaven on his encounter with the Bishop. She listened to Juan Diego's report and instructed him to return next morning.

Juan Diego returned home and found out that his uncle, Juan Bernardino was seriously ill. The local medicine man was called but soon it was evident that Juan Bernardino's fever was likely to take his life. Aztecs believed that the end of life was caused by one of the gods coming to take the soul of dying. So if one was hit by a bolt of lightning they believed that person was being called by Tlaloc. In this case, the shaman believed fever was a sign that the sun god was taking Juan Bernardino.

Of course, both Juan Bernardino and Juan Diego were Christians and had a different idea of how to deal with imminent death, a priest had to be called to administer the dying man the Sacrament of Last Rites.

Notice the image forming through the story, the sun is present in Juan Bernardino's illness as a fever, in Juan Diego's name as the morning's rising eagle, in the sunlight surrounding the Lady of Heaven, in Juan Diego's returning to Cuautitlan at sunset, and in many other smaller details. The eagle was a symbol representing nobility and greatness among the Aztecs. The whole story resounds with one message in the native mind: "the sun is here to visit us, to bring us light." We find that in the Old Testament, the Messiah is compared to great light dispelling darkness: "The people that walked in darkness, have seen a great light: unto those dwelling in the land of the shadow of death, light has shined."[75] St Matthew later quotes that: "the people who sat in darkness have seen a great light, and for those who sat in the region and shadow of death a light has dawned."[76] The prophecy of Isaiah

---

[75] See Isaiah 9:1-3.

is fulfilled in the Gospel According to St Matthew, indicating the beginning of Jesus' ministry in the land of Galilee. There, by Lake Gennesaret Christ is going to gather crowds and lead them to the light of truth by curing disease, expelling demons, and gathering large crowds hungry to hear the Word of God. The Mother of God was going to act very similarly to evangelize Mexico. People like Juan Bernardino were cured by the shores of Lake Texcoco, Mexico's Gennesaret; there the bloodthirsty demonic gods were expelled from the land, and millions of Mexicans were called to the light of Christ by the example of Juan Diego, and the message of Our Lady of Guadalupe. The three and a half days of the cycle of Guadalupe remind us of the Passion of the Christ. Juan Diego has to bring a message from Heaven to incredulous ears, and like so many other servants of Christ through the ages, he has to struggle with indifference and aggression to bring light to those dwelling in spiritual darkness. He is the vessel, a living Cuauhxicalli rising with the sacrifice of a pure heart, carrying with him the hopes of his people so the light won't be extinguished among them. He rises heavenward, struggling against the forces of darkness as a new St Paul, a new apostle to the Mexicans: "For our combat is not against blood and flesh, but against the rulers, against the authorities, against the principalities of this present darkness, against the spiritual forces of evil in the heavenly places."[77]

The third sunrise

Why was Juan Bernardino so ill at a time when Juan Diego was so busy dealing with those extraordinary errands from Heaven? We find the answer in the Gospel of John. There the disciples ask Jesus why a certain man had been born blind. Jesus' answer is clear, the man's defect was not an outward manifestation of a secret sin by him or his parents; it was an opportunity to show God's mercy working to rescue mankind from original sin and all its consequences. At the beginning of that passage only Jesus "can see" the situation. The disciples are "in the dark" and ask Jesus to explain who was responsible for the poor man's blindness. The blind man – in addition to his own physical blindness – is as much "in the dark" as the disciples. Those who can see must work while daylight lasts before night falls. In this brief parable, Jesus compares himself to the sun, giving light and life to the world. Many detractors of Christianity try to dismiss the Gospel as "just another solar myth"[78] but they cannot dismiss the realities attached to it. While it is true that human imagination has created myths throughout history, only God operates in such a way that he can direct creation to represent what he wants

---

[76] See Matthew 4:12-23.

[77] Ephesians 6:12.

[78] See *The Power of Myth* by Joseph Campbell. Published by Anchor Books, Random House.

to teach mankind. To use the well-known words of the British apologist C.S. Lewis: "Now the story of Christ is simply a true myth: a myth working on us in the same way as the others, but with this tremendous difference that it really happened."[79] The same thing is true of the story we read in the *Nican Mopohua* about Juan Diego, who is presented as a living Cuauhxicalli, carrying not the heart of a poor victim of the Aztec priests but the life of Christ in him. Juan Diego is given the task or being an example of Christ before his own people so they can also have light and life.

Chapter 9 of the Gospel According to St John begins with: "As he walked along, he saw a man who was born blind. His disciples asked him, 'Rabbi, who sinned, this man or his parents, that he was born blind?' Jesus responded, 'neither this man nor his parents sinned; he was born blind so that the works of God might be revealed in him. I must work the works of Him who sent me while there is daylight because night is coming when no one can work. As long as I am in the world, I am the light of the world.'"[80]

All Christian disciples are called to be the light of the world in imitation of Christ himself. "Jesus said, 'I came into this world for judgment so that those who do not see may see, and those who do see may become blind.'"[81] In the fifth chapter of the Gospel According to St Matthew, Jesus says: "You are the light of the world. A city built on a hill cannot be hidden. No one after lighting a lamp puts it under the bushel basket, but on the lamp-stand, and it gives light to all in the house.   In the same way, let your light shine before others, so that they may see your good works and give glory to your Father in heaven."[82] Who could deny that Juan Diego was chosen to bring the light of Christ, to be a "city built on a hill" to let the light of Christ shine before the whole Mexican nation born in unity at the Cerrito?

Juan Bernardino's illness was not an inconvenience. It was part of the sign presented to Juan Diego first, to the Zumarraga second, and to the Mexican people in the same way that the blind man in the Gospel of John, or the son of Gil Cordero. Later on, we will find that Juan Bernardino was trusted to remember the name of "Guadalupe" – a word his ears had never heard up to the moment of his miraculous cure.

---

[79] "Now the story of Christ is simply a true myth: a myth working on us in the same way as the others, but with this tremendous difference that it really happened: and one must be content to accept it in the same way, remembering that it is God's myth where the others are men's myths [...] At any rate I am now certain (a) That this Christian story is to be approached, in a sense, as I approach the other myths. (b) That it is the most important and full of meaning. I am also nearly certain that it really happened." C.S. Lewis *Letter to Arthur Greeves*, October 18, 1931.
[80] John 9:1-5.
[81] John 9:39.
[82] Matthew 5:14-16.

Juan Diego left that morning earlier than usual and tried to avoid meeting the Lady from Heaven on his way to the city. He did not remember that all mothers know what their children are up to. This part of the story reveals the child-like nature of Juan Diego. He loved his uncle and had to take care of his urgent needs. At the same time, he was planning to take care of the Lady's errand at a later date. To avoid a delay he took a different route that time but as he was passing by the Cerrito he saw the Lady coming down the slope. Our friend is no Prophet Jonah, he is not trying to escape from his duties as a messenger for the Virgin Mary but he feels he has failed twice to convince the Bishop and now – due to circumstances he cannot control – he is failing to receive from the Virgin Mary the promised proof of her presence. We understand his sincere apologies before the Lady of Heaven, he is still afraid of punishment, yet nothing of that sort is going to happen. Instead of a chastisement, Juan Diego hears the most beautiful words of consolation in the sweet sounds of his own language:

"Listen, put it into your heart, my little, most dear son, what has that frightened you, what has afflicted you is nothing. Do not let that disturb you. Do not fear this illness nor any other illness, nor any sharp and hurtful thing. Am I not here, I, who am your mother? Aren't you under my shadow and protection? Am I not the source of your joy? Aren't you in the hollow of my mantle, in the crossing of my arms? Do you need anything more?"[83]

While she is speaking these tender words of consolation to Juan Diego, she is also appearing to Juan Bernardino, telling him: "I am Saint Mary of Guadalupe, go to the Bishop and tell him all that you have seen and heard."[84] At the same time, she is telling Juan Diego: "Do not fear death, illness, or any sharp thing", in a clear reference to the dreaded sacrificial knife of the Aztec priests. Then she instructs Juan Diego to go to the top of the hill to gather flowers, she tells him to cut them and bring them back to her. At this point, Juan Diego must have thought, "another impossible task!" Now we know that was the first day of winter. The wind in Mexico at that time of the year comes from the north. Juan Diego knew that finding flowers at the hilltop was as impossible as it has been to convince the Bishop but he obediently commanded his old bones to climb the rest of the way to the top of the Tepeyac. The vision that had started with the beautiful song of birds was going to produce now another miracle. He found plenty of beautiful flowers and filled his ayate with them as instructed, descending the slope to where the Lady of Heaven was waiting for him. He had collected Castilian roses, flowers unknown in the American continent at the time. The Bishop would recognize them because he was a Spaniard, and a Franciscan well acquainted with Our

---

[83] *Nican Mopohua*, 119.

[84] "And that he would properly name her beloved Image thus: the Perfect Virgin, Holy Mary of Guadalupe." *Nican Mopohua*, 228.

Blessed Mother preference for beautiful roses. Our Lady tenderly arranged the flowers in a motherly gesture and instructs Juan Diego to show them to no one else but the Bishop.

Juan Diego walked the long road to the Bishop's residence only to be ill received. He was told to seat and wait. It was cold and he did not even have the cover of his tilma, now used to wrap the flowers. He sat there for three or four hours. Eventually, the guards asked him what was he carrying there. Juan Diego recalled the instructions of Our Lady, "show them to no one else but the Bishop" and tried to comply but the guards attempted to grab the flowers. Every time they tried, the roses dematerialized and appeared to be part of the tilma, as if painted or embroidered on the fabric.

The poor guards were most likely uneducated and superstitious men. They thought some kind of sorcery was going on. They had followed Juan Diego only a few days before and saw him disappear while crossing the causeway but this new trick was too much for them. Terrified they burst into the Bishop's chambers. Don Zumarraga was busy, perhaps with a family group after a baptismal ceremony. He allowed the guards to bring Juan Diego into the audience chamber. Juan Diego announced to the translator that he had the proof the Bishop requested. He was told to show it at once.

Juan Diego was in front of the Bishop, who was surrounded by a group of people. According to the information we have, there were some servants, the guards, the Franciscan translator, may be other religious, and a family group. Divine Providence arranged a varied group of witnesses to be present.

Juan Diego had tied two corners of the shorter side of his oblong poncho around his neck— the same tilma seen by millions of faithful over the last five centuries. He let go of the other end thus unloading the flowers on the ground. Of course, Juan Diego could not easily see the surface of the cloth, and besides, his eyes were most likely fixed on the Bishop and the translator with whom he was speaking. The impossible winter flowers from across the Atlantic spread about the floor. The image then appeared on the tilma that was just a nondescript piece of ayate only seconds before. It was at that point when the prophecy of Our Lady of Guadalupe to Juan Diego was fulfilled: "And know for certain that I will appreciate it exceedingly and reward it, that I will enrich you because of it, I will exalt you."[85] The poor Macehualtin stood there, as amazed as Don Juan de Zumarraga, Bishop of Mexico, and representative of King Charles V, King of Spain and Emperor of the Holy Roman Empire, humbly kneeled

---

[85] *Nican Mopohua*, 35.

before him, weeping and asking forgiveness for not having believed his words. The image of Our Lady of Guadalupe had entered the world and was already transforming hearts.

Flowers from heaven

Do not forget the flowers because they are very important. The poor souls selected for the cruel sacrifices at the altars of the Aztec gods were flowers harvested at the Xochiyaoyotl, the flower wars. Those wars were organized in a fashion similar to today's sports leagues competitions to capture men to be sacrificed to the gods. Those captured by both sides were destined to die at the altar. The Aztec gods demanded the sacrifices of those worshiping them but the Christian God was one that had willingly sacrificed himself for his people.

The flowers spread on the floor at the feet of Our Lady's image had a powerful symbolic charge. On the lower part of Our Lady's garment, heavenly hands had painted a shadow that clearly resembled the Crucified God. The girdle or bow around Our Lady's waist was a sign of her pregnancy. The bow appears as the nahui ollin, the flower of the sun. The image represents fertility; Our Lady of Guadalupe appeared to the natives "blooming" with the promise of life, she was a pregnant princess as indicated by the position of her delicate bow and the slight swelling of her abdomen. And yet – there was no skull next to it symbolizing death – her child was not condemned to a natural death like the children of Coatlicue Toniatzin.

For the Franciscans present at the scene of the miracle, the flowers had also a very strong meaning. They were familiar with a piece of Catholic history very connected with the miraculous sign happening before them. The Friars were surely reminded of Saint Didacus, better known as St Diego of Alcala, (1400-1463) the same saint that the Spanish monks honored in the 16th century when they named a village in California, now the city of San Diego. Yes, this was the very saint from whom Juan Diego took his confirmation name. The names of the Saints he chose for his new Christian identity were St John and St Diego. St John is usually depicted as "the eagle"[86]

---

[86] See Revelation 4: 6-7 where the four creatures give glory to God. Those are traditionally understood to represent the Four Evangelists in this order: St Mark, St Luke, St Matthew, and St John – "Around the throne, and on each side of the throne, are four living creatures, full of eyes in front and behind: the first living creature is like a lion, the second living creature is like an ox, the third living creature has a face like a human face, and the fourth living creature is like a flying eagle." The eagle is the symbol used to represent John the Apostle, the Evangelist who gave us the Fourth Gospel. His writing soars towards heaven like a mystical eagle seeking the light and divinity of Christ. In art, St John the Evangelist is often depicted with an eagle, symbolizing the heights he reached in writing his Gospel. St John was also "the Lord's beloved disciple" (John 21:7) – that is the same Nahuatl name Our Lady calls our beloved Juan Diego, "Juan-tzin"! During the

and St Diego is usually is represented carrying something hidden in his cloak: either roses or food for the poor. He was a doorkeeper in various convents and he used to give to the poor everything he could.

The traditional story tells that one day he was taking food to a poor beggar when he ran into his Superior, a very stern disciplinarian who asked him what was he carrying in the fold of his cloak. Very scared, poor St Diego answered that he was carrying some roses. When his Superior told him to open the cloak several dozen roses cascaded down to the floor.[87]

The similarity of his story with that of Juan Diego Cuauhtlatoatzin is obvious. What is not so obvious is that the miracle of the roses happened and was known one hundred years before Juan Diego was baptized selecting "Diego" for his Christian name.

For the astonished Franciscans watching the Guadalupe event unfold, that was a hidden miracle revealing that Our Lady was already working in the life of Juan Diego even at the time he was baptized. Our Lady of Guadalupe was sending a message to her Franciscan Friars: she had seen in Juan Diego the exemplary spiritual disposition of St Diego of Alcala, a man full of mercy and care for the poor. The message was coming through a poor Macehualtin they had been mistreating for the last four days. Now we can understand the tears, and deep apologies Don Juan de Zumarraga and his friars expressed before Juan Diego.

The vision described in the *Nican Mopohua* expands in all directions. It carries a message that is particularly directed to certain groups of people – the Spaniards, the Mexicans, and even people who were not yet born in 1531 – and also a universal message reassuring mankind of the tender love of Our Mother and Our Lord. One could analyze and contemplate the wonders of Guadalupe for a lifetime, and yet discover it anew every time. In my mind that is the clear signature of the Divinity.

Last Supper, the young Evangelist leaned against Jesus' chest and heard the heartbeat of the Most Sacred Heart. That is why St John is considered an example of how to listen to the life of God in all creation. In the same manner, the Cycle of Tepeyac begins with Juan Diego's auditory experience, listening in awe to the song of the birds of Heaven, and the glorious counterpoint of the mountain itself. Both clearly represent the totality of creation: Heaven and Earth.

[87] The Catholic Church remembers St Diego of Alcala on November 13.

7

THE IMAGE

The icon presented to us in St Juan Diego's tilma is fraught with meaning, loaded with enough signs to befuddle even the most perspicacious analyst. Many talented scholars have studied the image of Our Lady of Guadalupe to gain some understanding about the many symbolic layers contained in it. Obviously, we are contemplating a great mystery that will take generations to unfold. We have no other option but to "stand on the shoulders" of those scholars who came before us and continue their work. One could say that the whole experience of Guadalupe has its own semiosis,[88] its own mode of signification that exceeds the limits of its iconic representation and enters history itself, using people, languages, nations, and even the heavenly constellations to convey a message so rich in meaning and so simple in its soteriology: "Am I not here, I, who am your Mother?" That is not a rhetorical question. Our Lady of Guadalupe is simply stating that if we accept her as our mother she will "give us her Son" to effect our eternal salvation.

When Juan Bernardino was ill and waiting for death to come, Juan Diego had to go and find a priest to assist his beloved uncle. He was on his way to church when he ran into the Lady from Heaven. It was then when she uttered the now famous words of consolation: "Am I not here, I, who am your Mother?" The words of the Lady echoed Jesus' words from the Cross recorded by John the Evangelist: "When Jesus saw his mother and the disciple whom he loved standing beside her, he said to his mother, 'Woman, here is your son.' Then he said to the disciple, 'Here is your mother.' And from that hour the disciple took her into his own home."[89] For Mary Mother of God, her very motherhood is the fulfillment of a divine commandment: "Be a Mother to my beloved disciples." At Calvary, John represents all the faithful disciples that will ever be, and Mary is the Mother of all disciples from

---

[88] **Semiosis** (*Gr.* σημείωσις, sēmeíōsis) is a process that creates, assigns, or modifies signs, the generation of meaning. Charles Sanders Peirce (1839-1914) defines it as the interpretation of signs in reference to objects, sign interrelations, or semiotics.

[89] John 19:26-27.

that very moment.

After the events of 1531, all Mexicans received the image and message of Our Lady of Guadalupe into their homeland and she gave them peace. Throughout Christian history, there have been always iconoclasts who shun the use of images in religious practice, basing their actions on a literal and limited interpretation of the Second Commandment. Many Christian apologists over the centuries have effectively refuted that erroneous belief. Here we will only say that images have been rightly used by God to teach and even cure his people. One well-known example is the image made by Moses to save the Israelites from the bites of poisonous snakes: "The people approached Moses and said, 'We have sinned by murmuring against the Lord and against you; pray to the Lord to take the serpents away from us.' So Moses prayed for the people. And the Lord instructed Moses, 'Make [the likeness of] a poisonous serpent, and set it on a staff; and everyone who is bitten shall look at it and live'. So Moses fashioned a serpent of bronze and put it on a staff, and when a serpent bit someone, that person would look at the serpent of bronze and live."[90]

That account found in the book of Numbers was later used by Jesus to exemplify his own being "lifted up" nailed to a Roman cross: "And just as Moses lifted up the serpent in the wilderness, so must the Son of Man be lifted up, that whoever believes in him may have eternal life."[91]

Rivers of theological ink have flowed to comment those verses but we will concentrate on how Moses' Bronze Serpent and the Cross of Calvary parallel the lifting of the miraculous image before the humble Mexican people of 1531.

For starters, the image raised in the desert was a bronze reproduction of something real that was harming the people. Moses was instructed to make that image while God gave it a special power: anyone looking at the bronze snake could be healed from the bites of the real snakes. The sign "meant" healing. The Israelites admitted that the serpents were God's punishment for their own sin. Many centuries later, Christ would use that account as a parable of his own mission: to be lifted up crucified for the sins of the people. As the bronze copy of the snake neutralized the snake's venom, Christ, a perfect image of Adam neutralized the poison of original sin by being lifted up on the Cross in view of all the people. The principle is clear: God fights sinful fire with holy fire.[92] These examples point also to God and man working together for the salvation of the whole human race.

Here is where we have to recall the figure of Coatlicue Toniatzin, the Mother Earth of Aztec mythology. She was "the one dressed in a skirt made

---

[90] Numbers 21:8-9.

[91] John 3:14.

[92] *Strong's Exhaustive Concordance*: Fiery serpent, *seraph,* from *saraph*; burning, i.e. figuratively a poisonous serpent; specifically, a *saraph* or symbolical creature from their copper color, *seraph*. Curiously enough, the Hebrew word שָׂרָף [*Seraph*] is the same for "snake" and "fire".

of snakes" but she also was the one reminding mortals that everyone that lives must one day die without remedy. In the same manner that Moses' bronze snake neutralized the poison of the real snakes, Our Lady of Guadalupe came to neutralize the poison of the devilish gods, the bloodthirsty spawn of Coatlicue, mother of all the Aztec gods.

When Our Lady of Guadalupe came to evangelize the people of Mexico, she chose to appear before them as a Mother, speaking their own language, using some of the symbols of their religion, gently putting aside what was wrong and keeping what was good as St Paul once counseled the Thessalonians.[93]

Following the example of Moses and Jesus, God presents us with the image of Our Lady of Guadalupe on Tepeyac Hill where the temple of Coatlicue Toniatzin once stood. In doing so, Our Blessed Mother occupied the territory once ruled by demons and claimed it as her own by right of conquest. She had done the same all across the Middle East, Asia, and Europe where Christians gradually turned the old pagan basilicas dedicated to Venus Aphrodite, Diana Artemis, or Ceres Bona Dea, into Christian temples. Mary of Nazareth was now coming to claim her Mexican children and cure them of the effects of the venomous Aztec doctrine. For that purpose, she made herself a model of a Mother. In the same way, Christ came as a man to save us: "God made Him who knew not sin to be sin on our behalf so that in Him we might convert to the righteousness of God."[94]

As we delve deeper and deeper into the many signs presented to the Mexicans in the tilma of Juan Diego, we will realize that the image is the amoxtli[95] presented to them by Heaven, a Divine Codex designed to convert them to Christ.

Here is when our capacity to marvel is challenged. Anyone can see that a 16th-century ayate cannot naturally survive five centuries. Of course, the skeptics will automatically assume a succession of images re-created from time to time by the "wicked" Church to ensnare the simple Mexicans; that is their first, and perhaps the most honest, of the many objections they present. The simple child-like honesty of the story of Juan Diego, the many authorities that have examined the tilma through the years, and the sincere conversion of

---

[93] Thessalonians 5:20-21 – "Do not despise prophesying, but test everything; hold fast what is good, abstain from every form of evil."

[94] 2Corinthians 5:21 – "For our sake [God] made him be sin who knew no sin so that in him we might become the righteousness of God."

[95] "A Codex is a pre-Conquest or early Colonial document record composed of pictures, an *amoxtli*, painted by Indian *tlacuilos*, painter-scribes, on a long strip of fan-folded paper made from maguey fibers or the bark of a wild fig tree." *The Sacred Image is a ... Divine Codex*, article by Janet Barber, I.H.M. included in *A Handbook on Guadalupe*, published by the Franciscan Friars of the Immaculate, New Bedford, Massachusetts, 1997. ©Academy of the Immaculate.

so many skeptics—yours truly included—should suffice to counter those who have pooh-poohed the miraculous preservation of the ayate far beyond its natural limits. Of course, God—who lives outside of time—has built into the image a series of proofs that no human being could possibly falsify; those will become apparent as we examine their specific messages.

To my mind, the most impressive element is something that I would call "the Aleph of Mary"[96] because it reminds me of *The Aleph*, a famous short story by J. L. Borges. There the protagonist discovers a point in space that contains all other points. Anyone looking into Borges' Aleph could clearly see the whole universe at once in all its instances of space and time. Something similar seems to happen with the image miraculously impressed on Juan Diego's tilma. As the Israelites could "look at the image" of the bronze snake and be healed by the power of God, Mexico was also healed by looking at Our Lady of Guadalupe. The numerous signs contained in that image of the Virgin Mary would continue to be a matter of contemplation and reflection in the centuries to come. The image contains what appears to be an infinite number of spiritual treasures. It is imbued with the power of God.

For the Christian mind, the Cross will always be a sign of salvation, not of condemnation. Moses' Bronze Serpent is a copy, an image of a real snake; and the Cross (*Gr.* "stavros") is the counterpart of the Tree of Knowledge of Good and Evil (*Gr.* "stavros" in the *Septuagint*). In both cases (snake bites, original sin) a bad thing is defeated by its own reflection. The reflection is a sign that God has endowed with the power to destroy that bad thing. In the same manner, as the tilma "reflected" the attributes of Coatlicue Toniatzin, the natives could recognize that immediately. They also recognized that the evil qualities of Coatlicue were removed, and this new Mother was not only gentle, tender, and pure; she was also a powerful healer that could return her people to life. Unlike Coatlicue, Our Lady of Guadalupe was not killing her own sons. That becomes evident from the way the Perfect Virgin Mary deals with the failure of Juan Diego to deliver her message effectively. There Juan Diego represents all of us imperfect men, always falling short when trying to do the right thing. The natives observe that Mother Nature could be quite a generous mother but was also unforgiving with those who missed her cues. Mary of Guadalupe appeared to Juan Diego not as a demanding life-taking goddess but as a merciful life-giving Mother. The natives took notice. They were expecting the "Age of the Fifth Sun," something that would eventually

---

[96] *Aleph* is the first letter of the Hebrew Alphabet. The original pictograph of the letter was the idealized head of an ox that later evolved to a staff (the Hebrew letter ל *lamed*) combined with the original ox head to signify God, strong authority, or the head of a tribe. The modern form of the letter in Hebrew א is sometimes compared to a man plowing a field. Mystically is said to represent a man pointing with one arm up to Heaven and the other to Earth thus indicating that Earth is meant to reflect Heaven.

transform the very rules of nature; a world of mercy and love was replacing the cruel reality they were forced to live in. Our Lady of Guadalupe asked not for the hearts of her children to be cruelly extracted with a knife, instead, she asked them to consecrate their hearts to her with love and merciful deeds. Juan Diego was the model she selected: a humble man known for living a life of service to others.

The beautiful face of Mary is the most touching feature of the image. She is barely smiling, like a mother who is watching over a child recovering from some illness. Sister Lucy of Fatima had the perfect words to describe her maternal feelings: "tender sorrow." No one would have described Coatlicue and her priests with those words. The image of Our Lady of Guadalupe is saying "I am like you, I will take care of you, I am your Mother."

The Speaking Eagle

Juan Diego, the visionary of Tepeyac is part of the symbolic complexity of the story of Guadalupe. He was a resident of Cuautitlan, a forest that was located a few miles northwest of Tenochtitlan. His native name, Cuauhtlatouac means "speaking eagle" or "he who speaks like an eagle". He was among the first natives to be baptized. Perhaps his Catechist associated his name with St John the Apostle, the Eagle[97] and one of the Sons of Thunder.[98] Both share the name John, derived from the Hebrew name Yochanan. meaning "God is gracious". As we have seen in previous chapters, John the Apostle and Juan Diego had visions where the supernatural realities presented themselves as precious stones reflecting the glory of God. In the Revelation, John was invited to "go up" just as Juan Diego was invited to climb the Tepeyac. Both of them hear music before ascending; John hears trumpets, and Juan Diego hears birds singing in counterpoint with music coming from the mountain itself. St John in the Revelation: "After this, I looked, and there in heaven a door stood open! And the first voice, which I had heard speaking to me like a trumpet, said, 'Come up here, and I will show you what must take place after this.'" While St John is shown the Throne of God in all his splendor, Juan Diego is shown a glorified Tepeyac where even the common plants of the region shine transformed into beautiful jewels reflecting heavenly light. Both

---

[97] Revelation 4:7 – "The first living creature was like a lion, the second like a calf, the third had a face like a man, and the fourth was like an eagle in flight." These four creatures are traditionally understood to be the Four Evangelists, the "eagle in flight" representing St John the Apostle.

[98] Matthew 4:13-17 – [Jesus] went up the mountain and called to him those whom he wanted, and they came to him. And he appointed twelve apostles to be with him, and to be sent out to proclaim the Gospel, and to have the authority to cast out demons. So he appointed the twelve: Simon whom he named Peter, James son of Zebedee, and John the brother of James to whom he gave the name *Boanerges*, which means "sons of thunder".

visions announce the future blessings that God will bestow upon mankind when the world is once again free of sin and wickedness. The throne that St John sees in his vision is something much more glorious than the throne of Zeus-Jupiter that used to be one of the Seven Marvels of the ancient world in his time. In the same manner, Juan Diego contemplates Tepeyac with a glory that never existed when the temple of Coatlicue stood there. Both visionaries are allowed to peek into a future age. Since the Aztecs were expecting the Age of the Fifth Sun, that expectation fit the hopes of the natives perfectly. The Perfect Virgin Santa María de Guadalupe was seamlessly joining two worlds and two ages. Even that was evident to the Mexican mind by the way the tilma was sewn together. The seam aptly represented a division between "before and after" with the gracious face of Mary confidently gazing into the future, her hands joined in a clapping gesture, and her left knee raised as if she was stepping forward in a joyful, dance-like step.

The story develops along four successive mornings, December 9 to December 12. It is important to remember that in 1531, the Church celebrated the Immaculate Conception on December 9—today, Catholics observe that feast on December 8. The native Mexicans were preparing to celebrate the day of the Winter Solstice—December 12—the day of the sun god. They believed that four suns had existed in four previous ages, and all of them had died at the end of each age. The arrival of the Spaniards and the end of the ancient imperial order was proof enough for them that a new era was dawning.

The native name of Juan Diego "the one who talks like an eagle" surely did not go unnoticed to the natives hearing the story of Our Lady's apparitions for the first time. He was the *Cuauhxicalli*, the eagle that struggled heavenward taking the offerings to the sun-god. The new parable fit perfectly in the native mind: Cuauhtlatouac spoke to them with the authority of the Eagle, the greatest of all the gods. He met the Perfect Santa Maria de Guadalupe, the Mother of God. A new age was just starting, she wanted to be a Mother to them just like Coatlicue had been in past ages. But this new mother was powerful, she could heal, she had ended the human sacrifices and the flower wars. Cuauhtlatouac— a native just like them—was her messenger, one that was chosen to speak the word of God with dignity even to the Spanish Priests. Did not the Bishop himself kneel before him, weeping, and begging forgiveness?

Obviously, it is very difficult to know what went through the natives' minds as the story of Juan Diego was told and heard by millions. What we really know is that the natives found a new dignity in the newly arrived Christian order. Perhaps that is the reason why the Perfect Virgin Mary decided to unite Spain and Mexico under the advocation of Santa Maria de Guadalupe. Like many other mothers had done through the ages, she was teaching her children how to get along.

The Impossible Canvas

A typical tilma or ayate is made of maguey cactus fibers known as *ixtle*, woven on a backstrap loom. Typically, to make the basic material, the flesh of the plant is removed, exposing the fibers that are later combed, washed, dried, and spun into a yarn. It is a very coarse material similar to burlap but very durable and sturdy.

Juan Diego's ayate is made of two separate pieces sewn together with a cotton thread. The two panels of cloth join slightly to the left of Our Lady's head. The seam is very visible and runs vertically along the length of the cloth, dividing it into two sections roughly equal in size. Around 1531, native men wore a wide loincloth, sandals, and a tilma. The tilma had many uses. Men could use it as a cloak, or as a bag to carry things.

The fabric only lasts a few years under normal wear but carefully stored may last up to two or three decades. The tilma with the image of Our Lady has maintained its structural integrity and plasticity without any sign of deterioration for nearly five centuries. Its two pieces are about 70 by 40 inches.[99] Juan Diego's cloak has rejected insects and microorganisms such as fungus and bacteria. For some unknown reason, it also rejects dust and other contaminants present in the air.

An important part of the Miracle of Tepeyac is that no one can explain how the tilma survived to this day. The material should have deteriorated long ago. Many skeptics affirm—without any proof—that the miracle is an ongoing scam, that the tilma is simply replaced periodically. That affirmation has been debunked many times in many ways but some continue to repeat it.

Miguel Cabrera,[100] the famous Mexican painter, was allowed to study Juan Diego's tilma. He made various copies of the image.[101] He is the author of *American Marvel*,[102] a report for the *Colegiata de Guadalupe* where Cabrera applied his expertise to analyze the image from a strictly artistic point of view. His naked eye examination concluded that parts of the image were realized in oil paint, others with egg tempera, and yet others, "al aguazo."[103] He was the first to observe that the sun rays surrounding the image were painted with a technique that made them appear to be part of the tilma fibers. He added that, to his knowledge, no artist had ever attempted to combine techniques in

---

[99] 105 cm by 168 cm.

[100] Miguel Mateo Maldonado y Cabrera (1695-1768).

[101] He was allowed to study the image of Our Lady of Guadalupe to make two copies: one for Archbishop José Manuel Rubio y Salinas, and one for Pope Benedict XIV. He copied a third to be used as a master in future reproductions.

[102] Original Spanish title: *Maravilla Americana y Conjunto de Raras Maravillas, Observadas con la Dirección de las Reglas del Arte de la Pintura en la Prodigiosa Imagen de Nuestra Señora de Guadalupe de Mexico*, by Miguel Mateo Maldonado y Cabrera. Imprenta Real del Más Antiguo Colegio de San Ildefonso, 1756.

[103] **Aguazo, gouache:** a technique of painting with opaque watercolors prepared with gum.

such manner. He also noted that someone capable of such a feat would never choose to work on a surface so coarse and inadequate as ayate.

One skeptic was an Austrian atheist, physicist, and chemist, Dr. Richard Kuhn, who won the 1938 Nobel Prize in Chemistry for his work on carotenoids and vitamins. In 1936, Dr. Kuhn was given two minuscule fibers of the tilma for examination. He was told nothing about their origin. He correctly dated their age to the 16th century but he could not match the colors to any known kind of pigmentation of animal, vegetable, or mineral origin. Using a spectrophotometer he determined that, whatever the pigment was, it did not exist in the periodical table of elements. After the analysis was completed, Dr. Kuhn requested to know the origin of those fibers. He was told they came from the tilma of Juan Diego, the visionary of Tepeyac. Of course, Dr. Kuhn did not know a thing about Juan Diego or the Miracle of Tepeyac but he visited Mexico several times and eventually investigated the matter in more detail. That resulted in his conversion to the Catholic Faith. He died a faithful Catholic in Heidelberg, Germany in 1967. Juan Diego's tilma had won a convert through faith and reason.

The Symbols of Guadalupe

The image imprinted on Juan Diego's tilma was seen by the native Mexicans as *amoxtli*, that is a codex created by a scribe or *tlahcuilo*. Codices registered stories, history, and other important events on a deerskin, or a foldable sheet of paper made of tree-bark or some other available fiber. Thanks to the work of scholars like Fr Mario Rojas Sanchez, the symbols and meaning contained in the tilma are now gradually coming to life after centuries of studies. In my personal view, after a few years of contemplating the image and reading about its meaning, is that Juan Diego's ayate speaks by means of its own semiosis, obviously owning its own process of signification, a process combining the canon developed by the ancient Mesoamerican cultures with the no less ancient Christian Byzantine canon that gradually developed in the Orient from the days of St Luke. I would like to approach one specific view here, that the image of Our Lady of Guadalupe is perhaps a very important part of a more complex system of symbols presented to the believers of every age since the days when St Luke carved the first image of Our Lady of Guadalupe, the one now being venerated at the Monastery of the same name in Extremadura, Spain.

Dom. Columban Hawkins, O.C.S.O., reports a very interesting anecdote in his essay *An Iconography of Guadalupe*: "Yet, strangely enough, when a Russian Orthodox Priest, Fr A. Ostrapovim, Dean of the Chair of Church Archeology in Moscow, and unacquainted with the history of Our Lady of Guadalupe, was presented with a copy of this picture for approval, he replied that this is an icon, definitely of the Byzantine type and presumably of Eastern-Asiatic origin. It was his opinion that the painter of this Icon deviated from the very severe canons of icon painting and introduced much of himself into it."[104] This precise analysis reinforces my idea that perhaps—and I must strongly warn you, dear reader, that this is only a personal impression—St Luke the Evangelist, from Heaven, may have been involved—from Heaven—in the creation of this icon, although it is quite clear that the inspiration comes from Our Blessed Mother, who is ultimately responsible for its creation. She is a Queen and she can commission a portrait from her favorite artist if she wants to.

The inspired author of the Gospel According to St Luke and the Acts of the Apostles may have started something much bigger than a simple account of Jesus' ministry and the early days of the Christian Church. According to well-documented traditions, he was the author of various portraits and carvings depicting Mary of Nazareth, including the one kept in Extremadura, and the painting of Our Lady of Częstochowa, kept at the Monastery of Jasna Góra,[105] among other works now dispersed throughout Europe. The Gospel of Luke—often called "The Gospel of Mary"—was sent to a man named Theophilus, appropriately called "friend of God"[106] and perhaps a providential sign that Luke's work was meant for all the people of God through the ages. That may have been the beginning of a Grand Cycle or parable meant to instruct the Church in future, more perilous times. Certainly, a collection of symbolic events, relics, writings, and saints spread through two millennia of history should encourage the faithful to trust that God is in control, that Our Lord is the Lord of History. He is painting, so to speak, the story of salvation on the canvas of space and time. Only God Almighty can do such things.

Having that in mind, we must look into the collection of signs presented to us by Our Lady of Guadalupe. However, we will not restrict our analysis only to the Sacred Image. We will look also at persons, dates, events, and any other meaningful things connected with the signs contained therein. It is a mighty collection meant to be discovered gradually, with messages for every

---

[104] *A Handbook on Guadalupe,* p. 63 "The Iconography of Guadalupe" article by Dom. Columban Hawkins, O.C.S.O. Published by the Franciscan Friars of the Immaculate, New Bedford, Massachusetts, 1996.

[105] Ancient documents state that the icon of Our Lady of Częstochowa came from Constantinople. There is a tradition telling that in 1384, Count Władysław Opolczyk was traveling through Częstochowa with the Icon when his horses refused to go on—a similar event occurred to those carrying the image of Our Lady of Luján, in 1630—in a dream, Władysław was instructed to leave the icon at Jasna Góra. The mantle covering Our Lady of Częstochowa is decorated with golden stars in a style similar to that of Our Lady of Guadalupe.

[106] *Gr.* Θεοφιλος "friend of God". See Luke 1:1-4. The first verses of that Gospel may have inspired the introduction of the *Nican Mopohua* for they are quite similar.

generation. From a distance of five centuries prepare to hear the voice of Our Lady calling us from the Tepeyac.

The Aleph of Mary

We are back before the image trying to think like the 16th century Mexicans who have been subjugated by foreigners. Their culture is alive in them but the invaders do not understand their rich heritage, and the little they can understand they despise as demonic superstition. Mary of Nazareth has come to save the Mexican race, and also to teach her Spanish children a lesson in mercy. From the deep reservoir of God's grace, she has to bring a message that will reach the Mexican mind in their terms and symbols, while concealing from the Spaniards those elements she is going to borrow from the Aztec culture to captivate the natives' hearts. The soldiers of Cortez had recoiled in horror before the human sacrifices, the ritual homosexuality of the priests, the horrible idols made with a paste concocted with corn and human blood, their ritual cannibalism, and their merciless flower wars. Our Lady had to find the way to speak to both cultures and bring them together. No diplomat will ever match her skill in making one Christian nation of such a motley crowd.

The holy angels are messengers of God. The word *angelos* (ἀγγελος, pronounced áng-eh-lohs) means "messenger" in Greek. The Aztec mythology did not include angels, that is why when the natives saw the angel depicted in the tilma, they thought it was Juan Diego. The angel is "bringing" Our Lady on his wings, Juan Diego's original name was "the one speaking like an eagle" and he was also the messenger of Our Lady, the one that brought "her breath, her words" to the Mexican people. The angel's wings are painted in three bands of red, white, and blue, associating them in the native mind with Tlaloc, the god of rain and thunder. The red color was normally associated with the edge of the sacrificial knife made of obsidian rock. This time the knife is not there, it has been replaced by harmless feathers. The end of the era of human sacrifices announced by Quetzalcoatl, the feathered serpent, is coming to an end.

The angel is depicted in motion, he is carrying Our Lady in one definite direction right-to-left. The angel with eagle wings is carrying the Queen from one fading age to a new age. The angel's face—like the face of Mary—is on the left side of the seam. To the native imagination, her hands are clapping, her left knee is advancing in the same direction. She is entering the "north" of the tilma—remember the Aztecs represented maps with the East up, West down, South to the right, and North to the left. In Mexico, the weather, the cold winter wind, all come from the northern quadrant. The apparition happened on the day of the Solstice of Winter, on the 13th day (*Acatl*, Reed) of the 1st month (*Cuauhtli*, Eagle) of the 4th age (*Tecpatl*, flint knife) when the days begin to grow longer and the sun (Tonatiuh) is reborn. Mary of Nazareth appears to them as a messenger of life, she is pregnant, she brings in her the promise of Spring.

The angel is holding her mantle (the sky) with his left hand and her garment (the earth) with his right. Her mantle is decorated with stars symbolizing Heaven. The turquoise cloak is the color of the quetzal bird. For the Aztecs, that was the color of Moctezuma's headdress and cloak—no one else was allowed to wear that color symbolizing the blessings of fertility brought by sun and rain. The meaning of the sign was clear: the Perfect Virgin Mary was now an Empress, she was a force for life and fecundity, she was like Coatlicue Toniatzin, the Mother of the Sun but she did not have those menacing claws, her feet were visible under the edge of her garment and they were shod with delicate slippers. Those looking at her picture after listening to Juan Diego's story could understand she was a loving Mother bringing new life and a new era of peace.

The color of Our Lady's cloak brought to the native mind the most sacred of birds, the quetzal. Its feathers of lush green were a sign of the fertile forests of Paradise "the land of flowers, the land of plentiful corn, of fleshly pleasures, the garden of abundance, the heavenly realms" that Juan Diego mentions in the *Nican Mopohua*.

Her cloak covers her pink outer garment. The red hue of Our Lady's garment is the color of Earth, the silk embroidery laying on top of her dress is decorated with three kinds of flowers. The largest of those flowers are called *tepetl*,[107] used by the scribes as a graphic symbol for mountains or hills. In 1981, Fr Mario Rojas Sanchez had an intuition about the large flowers seen in Our Lady's dress, and the stars depicted on her cloak. Basically, the mantle represents the sheltering Heavens and her dress represents the fruitful Earth. With the help of Dr. Juan Hernandez Illescas, the original intuition of Fr Rojas Sanchez led to some astonishing discoveries. First, they identified the flower that represents Tepeyac Hill. That is the only "mountain" without forestation on top. Using that point of reference, they created a transparency where the basic contour of the elements in the tilma was represented in the correct scale. They placed that transparency on the map of Mexico using the Aztec conventional orientation—East on top, as opposed to North on top as we are used to seeing maps in modern cartography—centering the Tepeyac so that the head of the image is on the Atlantic (East) side. When they did that they noticed that the nine *tepetl* flowers on her dress coincided roughly with the geographic position of a number of nine volcanoes and hills.

The second was the flower of Quetzalcoatl, an eight-petal flower used to symbolize Venus, the morning star. In Aztec mythology, there was the belief that Quetzalcoatl had turned into the morning star after he died. He was the god that had promised to return to claim his throne and end all human sacrifices. The third flower was the Nahui-Ollin symbolizing the union of all four natural elements: earth, wind, water, and fire; the four seasons, and also

---

[107] As in Popoca**tepetl**, the famous volcano in Mexico.

the four cardinal points. The four petals also represented the four ages that had passed, with its center representing the Fifth Sun to be born on the first day of Winter, when Our Lady produced the Miracle of the Tilma.

The four ages past were named in Aztec mythology. Nahui-Ocelotl, the first, was the Age of the Jaguar. This was the age of the giants who were devoured by jaguars as their world perished. Then came the Nahui-Ehecatl, the Age of the Wind. The people of that age were transformed into monkeys who perished when giant storms destroyed their world. Nahui-Quiahuitl was the Age of the Rain. The world of that age succumbed to fire, only birds could survive the firestorm. Nahui-Atl, the Age of Water. This age finished with a great flood that only fish could survive and only a few men survived but were transformed into dogs. Nahui-Ollin, the Age of Earthquakes. This is the present age that—according to Aztec mythology—will end when the world will be destroyed by a strong earthquake. Please compare with Revelation 11:13;[108] 8:1-5;[109] Haggai 2:6.[110]

Fr Mario Rojas Sanchez and Dr. Hernandez Illescas also believe that the stars in the mantle are a representation of the sky at the moment Juan Diego delivered "the sign" to Bishop Zumárraga on December 12, 1531. The stars appear "as a mirror image," as if the observer was outside the Universe looking in. Of course, that was neither done to confuse anyone nor to conceal the meaning. It was done on purpose because the Aztecs studied the stars by looking at them reflected in a pool of water where certain reference points could be used to detect the movement of the constellations—i.e. sticks or other markers placed on the edge of the pool. The stars are placed following the Aztec convention; East is up (where our North usually is), North is to the right (where our East is found in most maps). Using the stars of the mantle, one can project the stars that are not shown: the Boreal Crown is appropriately located right on the Virgin's head; Virgo is on her bosom, near her praying hands. Leo the Lion is in her womb, right above the Nahui-Ollin flower, also coinciding with Regulus, the "little king". This is the star that the Magi observed[111] in conjunction with Jupiter (the king of planets) on the constellation of Leo. The Lion is a symbol of Judah, the tribe of the Messiah as indicated in Genesis.[112] The unusual triple conjunction of the Planet King

---

[108] Revelation 11:13 – There was a great earthquake that lasted one hour, and a tenth of the city was destroyed. Seven thousand were killed in the quake, and the rest were terrified and gave glory to the God of Heaven.

[109] Revelation 8:1-5 – "Then the angel took the incensory and filled it with the fire of the altar, and cast it to the earth; there followed the roar of thunder, sounds, flashes of lightning, and an earthquake"

[110] Haggai 2:6 – Moreover, the Lord Almighty says: 'In just a short while I will once again shake the sky and the earth, the sea and the dry land.

[111] Matthew 2:2 – Where is he who has been born king of the Jews? For we have seen *his star* rise in the East, and we have come to worship him.

with the Little King Star in the constellation Leo, of the royal house of Israel, indicated to the Magi both by its odd appearance and its brilliance, that the man destined to be the King of the Jews was about to be born.[113] We can see Regulus and Leo in Mary's womb, next to the Nahui-Ollin the divine flower, at the time when the stars of the winter constellations indicate the birthday of the Sun, thirteen days before Christmas. Christ, the new Sun is to take the title of Lord of the Near and Far, right at the Solstice of Winter, at the beginning of the "trecena"[114] (the Solstice, near) and at the end (Christmas, far) on the 4-Tecpatl (the four petals of the Nahui-Ollin), of the 13-Acatl (the Christian year of 1531), and the 1-Cuauhtli (the Eagle). I imagine that the coincidence of all these elements is highly improbable, and I am also sure we are missing much more.

On the right side of her mantle—in Aztec iconography this would be the South—we see the southern constellations as they appeared on December 12, 1531. From top to bottom: Ophiuchus, Libra, Scorpio, Lupus, Hydra, Centaurus, and the Southern Cross, and finally Sirius, the lone star at the lower corner. Notice that the stars on her left arm appear to form a Rosary with the Southern Cross representing the small Crucifix at the end. Then on the left side, representing the North to the Aztecs, we find: Boötes, Ursa Major, Berenice's Mane, Canes Venatici (the Hounds). Below the constellations of Draco (the Dragon), Auriga, and Taurus are represented by some of their brightest stars. In total, forty-six of the brightest stars shining on the night sky over Mexico are there. It is hard not to draw a parallel between this image and the woman described by St John the Apostle in the 12th chapter of the Book of Revelation.

The greatest marvel of Our Lady of Guadalupe seems to be her capacity to generate a seemingly infinite number of signs in a sort of palimpsest of prodigies contained within the small space of Juan Diego's humble cloak. Certainly, Jorge Luis Borges' utterly fantastic *Aleph* is nothing compared to the miraculous tilma which has the advantage of being real.

Our Lady is also standing on a Black Moon. That may have been her way to mark the year. The natives were thus reminded of the solar eclipse that occurred on March 18, 1531. It also shows that her Son had conquered the powers of darkness, and the end of the struggle between light and darkness was near. Coyolxauhqui, the moon goddess had been vanquished by the Mother of Christ, the New Sun. The Nahuatl scholar, Miguel León-Portilla[115]

---

[112] Genesis 49:9 – Judah, you are a lion's cub; from the prey, my son, you have gone up. He stooped down, he couched as a lion, and as a lioness; who dares rouse him up?

[113] *The Star of Bethlehem*, a video by Rick Larson, and Stephen Vidano.

[114] Spanish for "thirteen days". The Aztecs had months of thirteen days and believed there were thirteen heavens, and nine underworlds—each representing one month of the human gestation period.

favors the etymology "navel of the moon" as the origin of the word for Mexico, following from moon, *metztli* and navel, *xictli*.

Virgin and Mother

The black ribbon tied high above her womb indicates she is pregnant in the same manner as Coatlicue though—unlike the pagan goddess—Mary's ribbon has two bows with four ends hanging. Black is the color of Quetzalcoatl who is sometimes depicted with a black ant on his nose. That symbolizes his power to turn himself into an ant to descend unnoticed into the underworld to give new life to the dead by giving them his own blood.

Our Lady of Guadalupe bows down modestly in a gesture full of tender mercy. The native gods were always looking forward with eyes wide open but mortals could not do that. It was considered bad manners for anyone who was not a priest or a male member of the high nobility. From the tilma, the Perfect Virgin Mary looks not imperiously at her people but with love and compassion. The face of Our Lady is that of a young girl. Today we would consider her a *Mestiza*, half Indian and half Spanish. There were not many children of mixed race in 1531. In a way, her demeanor is a prophetic look into the future. She is announcing the birth of a new race.

Her hair is combed as a maiden but she is pregnant. Aztec mores were such that a maiden was always meant to be a virgin—certainly not a common assumption in our early 21st century—but she has told Juan Diego who she was, "the Perfect Virgin Holy Mary, Mother of God." There is no contradiction between her virginity and her pregnancy. Here is the genius of the symbol presented to the Mexicans: it serves as a way to present them with the Gospel using the symbols of their own religion. I can imagine some of the natives asking: "How could a Virgin be also a Mother?" For those who already had the concept of the miraculous motherhood of Coatlicue Toniatzin,[116] it was not too difficult to accept the perpetual virginity of Mary, and the dogma of the Virginal Birth of Jesus.

Christians see Our Lady of Guadalupe and immediately assume that her hands are joined together in prayer because that is what Christians do. The signs presented to us show a wonderful duality. Her hands remind us of the

---

[115] Miguel León Portilla is Mexican scholar considered the world's foremost authority on Nahuatl philology and philosophy. He is a professor at the National Autonomous University of Mexico School of Philosophy and Letters since 1957, and Director of the Historical Research Institute. He is the author of *Tonantzin Guadalupe*. He holds an MA with distinction from Loyola University in Los Angeles and a Ph.D. from the National Autonomous University of Mexico (UNAM).

[116] In Aztec mythology, Coatlicue was supernaturally impregnated by a ball of feathers touching her while she was in her temple. That myth explained the conception of the demon Huitzilopochtli without the help of a father.

"casita", the chapel she wants to have on Tepeyac Hill. A church is, of course, a house of prayer. She also said she wanted to "give her son" to the people in that chapel. That expression is rich in meaning: she wants to give the people her Son, the God of light that is about to be born on that Winter Solstice. The Eucharist will be given to the faithful there, that is also her Son given to the faithful as the Bread from Heaven.

Many of the natives, in particular, the ones who were already attending Holy Mass, could look at the Virgin's hands and associate them with prayer. To those who were not quite familiar with Christian customs, she appeared to be clapping her hands, raising her left knee, and modestly looking down as she danced. The Sacred Image is artfully crafted to prepare the heart of those watching for the reception of the Christian doctrines.

There is an aura of light around her which the natives understood perfectly: it is in the nature of the Mother of the Sun to irradiate light. She is pregnant with and is about to give birth to "the God for Whom we all live". The position of the sacred flower, the Nahui-Ollin right on her womb further reinforces the Divine Nature living in her. Finally, the Cross adorning her neck, the only purely Christian sign in the whole *amoxtli* confirms to them that her Son is the Christian God that has triumphed over the bloodthirsty gods of the Aztec priests. A shadow on her tunic shows the Crucified: this is a God that sacrificed himself so that his people can live. He does not need his people to be sacrificed for him. The end of the human sacrifices has arrived in time for the age of the Fifth Sun.

Fr Luis Becerra Tanco, (1603-1672) was a Catholic priest and a historian, with extensive knowledge of native dialects. He once held the chair of astronomy at the Royal University of Mexico. In 1666, he published *The Miraculous Origin of the Sanctuary of Nuestra Señora de Guadalupe,*[117] a compendium of the testimony presented before the magistrates of the Holy Office examining the petition of a Feast date, and the office of Mass for Our Lady of Guadalupe. Among a wealth of information about the native customs, he explains in his opus that the scribes or *tlacuilos* would sign and date their work near the center of the lower edge of the *amoxtli*. I have noticed a small number 13 in Arabic numbers on Our Lady's vestment, slightly over the right thumb of the angel. It can be seen using a magnifying glass. The color of the edge of the mantle that the angel is holding is *matatlli*, almost the phonetic equivalent of *matatctli*, the word for "ten". The natives see the following representation: *Yei xictlali ipan matlcalli*—three stars on a green field—which read in a hieroglyphic manner is "three on top on ten" which is the way Aztecs expressed the number thirteen. Now 1531 was 13-Acatl in the Aztec calendar, that is "13-Reed". The Reed can be seen next to the thirteen,

---

[117] *Nuestra Señora De Guadalupe Y Origen De Su Milagrosa Imagen*, by Fr Luis Becerra Tanco, orig. publ. 1666; Imprenta y Litografia Española de Mexico, 1883.

touching Our Lady's foot. What appears to be the head of a fawn can be seen on the vestment, next to the corner of the mantle. The scribes often used a deerskin to draw their *amoxtli*.[118]

Finally, we have the halo. Our Lady appears before the sun but she does not eclipse the sun like the goddess Coyolxauhqui. She completely fits the description of the woman clothed with the sun, with the moon under her feet and a crown of twelve stars described by St John the Apostle in Revelation 12:1 – "A great sign appeared in the sky, a woman clothed with the sun, with the moon under her feet, and on her head a crown of twelve stars."

The picture aptly represents the triumph of Christ over the darkness of paganism. The rays—an attribute of the demon Huitzilopochtli—now belong to the New Sun that is Christ, Son of Mary. She is the Mother of Light, Mother of the Sun, the Perfect Ever Virgin Mother of the True God for whom we live.

The image of Our Lady of Guadalupe is a perfect parable that leaves the natives ready and eager to embrace their new Mother. In time this will help them form a new national identity as well, all in record time, only four decades after Columbus' arrival, and barely over two decades after the landing of Cortez on the shores of Yucatan.

The Windows to Her Soul

The eyes of Our Lady of Guadalupe are one of the great mysteries of all times. No artist has been able to duplicate her simple and yet mysterious gaze. From early on, many had affirmed that a bearded man could be seen reflected in her left eye. When optical technology finally caught up, several specialists have examined the ayate, confirming that the scene of the miracle is perfectly registered in her eyes. It would have been impossible for the best artist of the 16th century to paint that scene in that little space, on such a rough medium.

Those minute human figures could not possibly be painted by any artist in 1531. In that small space, scarcely eight millimeters wide. The eyes of Our Lady of Guadalupe reflect the scene of the miracle in two sections. In the first section appears Don Juan de Zumarraga in front of Juan Diego who is opening his ayate where the image had just appeared. There are other persons with him, a total of thirteen: the translator Juan Gonzalez, a black woman, a second man standing next to Zumarraga, yet another man on the opposite side who is grabbing his chin, and there is also a native musician sitting on the floor. The second section of the scene is in the center of the eyes where a couple can be seen. The woman is standing next to a child, and she is also

---

[118] See pp. 68-70 at the end of the subtitle "The Stars on Mary's Mantle," part of the essay by Dr. Janet Barber I.H.M. *The Sacred Image is ... a Divine Codex*, of *A Handbook on Guadalupe*, a collection of essays by various authors published by the Franciscan Friars of the Immaculate, New Bedford, Massachusetts, 1996.

carrying a baby in the manner typical of native women.

Thirteen people can be seen in total. It looks like the arrival of Juan Diego had interrupted a gathering after a baptism ceremony. Both sections of the scene are reflected in both eyes just like they would in normal human eyes. Using the latest scanning techniques available, scientists have been able to find the reflections of Juan Diego, Don Juan de Zumarraga, and eleven others. As I write this, at the end of June 2017, I have unconfirmed reports that, using nanotechnology,[119] an even more minute reflection of Juan Diego has been found inside the reflection, in one of the eyes of Bishop Zumarraga. Even with today's technology, it is impossible to reproduce such small images on such a rough surface using a brush.

The Mystery of Her Eyes Deepens

It was 1929 when a photographer, Alfonso Marcue Gonzalez, discovered a tiny human figure in the right eye of Our Lady of Guadalupe. That led others to investigate the image further as technology increased their ability to peer into ever smaller fields. Teams of ophthalmologists have examined the eyes of the sacred image, others have photographed it with the highest definition cameras at their disposal. Finally, in the late 1970s, a Peruvian scientist, a graduate of Cornell University employed by IBM Mexico, Dr. Jose Aste Tönsmann scanned some of the high definition photographs available. Commissioned by the Mexican Center for Guadalupan Studies, he was able to define the images of a total of thirteen persons, including the few that had been found previously.

Dr. Tönsman's most astonishing discovery was the second image of Juan Diego extending his tilma, reflected in one of the eyes of Don Juan de Zumarraga. The size of that image was on the order of $0.25\mu m$.[120] This is certainly an amazing discovery that leads us to an even more amazing conclusion: Our Lady of Guadalupe prepared this miracle to last in time so it could talk to believers of a more technologically advanced era. Mary of Nazareth's eyes are looking deep into the future while at the same time she extends an invitation to skeptics to sweetly accept her Queenship in the same way that others have done, like her Mexican children, and Dr. Richard Kuhn the Austrian, a Nobel Prize Winner in Chemistry who was also an Atheist Jew who surrendered like a child to the Miracle of Tepeyac and died a faithful Catholic.

---

[119] Nanotechnology is the area of science dealing with dimensions of less than 100 nanometers (0.0001mm), in particular, entities or phenomena at the molecular and submolecular level.

[120] A micron equals a millionth of a millimeter.

Juan Diego's 13

The experts have found the image of thirteen characters in the eyes of Our Lady. The same people are reflected in both the left and the right eye as it naturally happens in the eyes of any human being. The reflection appears to a snapshot of the moment when Juan Diego extends his tilma before Bishop Zumárraga on December 12, 1531, between 10 and 11 a.m.

There is no doubt that no one in the 16th century could have painted those images with that minuteness and precision. No artist of our age could reproduce those images without the help of cutting edge technologies. I doubt even with the technologies available in 2017 such images could be impressed on fibers of a quality similar to Juan Diego's tilma. Even if such a thing could be done, there is no way the iridescence of the image of Our Lady could be reproduced on a rough surface of similar quality. No one to this day could guarantee that the cloth would last five centuries under the same conditions endured by the image of Our Lady of Guadalupe.

The people reflected in her eyes—from left to right—include (1) a seated Indian, most likely a musician holding what appear to be two maracas. There is also (2) an elderly man who looks like Don Juan de Zumárraga, and (3) a younger white man, the translator Juan Gonzalez. There is (4) a native male wearing a cone-shaped hat, holding one edge of his tilma. That is obviously Juan Diego. (5) A dark-faced woman, (6) a black servant known to have been an African woman, a servant of the Bishop; and (7) one more Spaniard pensively holding his chin with his right hand. Those complete the peripheral area of the field of vision. The eyes are looking directly to a smaller, different group. It seems to me these are part of a family received by the Bishop after a baptism. They are a family of natives—from left to right—(8) a man, (9) a woman, (10) a young girl (11) a woman carrying (12) a baby on her back in the style of the natives, a (13) a young boy. All the way to the right we see Juan Diego again with his cone-shaped hat.

The scene confirms the story as related in the *Nican Mopohua*. The servants or guards that tried and failed to grab the flowers were startled when they saw them disappear into the tilma as if they were embroidered in the cloth. They were so scared that they burst into the Bishop's audience room where apparently a family was either in the process of baptizing a child or perhaps, after the baptism they were having a friendly chat with the Bishop. That agrees with the fact that Juan Diego is wearing a hat in the Bishop's presence. Most likely he was hastily dragged into the audience room and did not have time to respectfully remove his hat since his hands were busy holding the tilma. Being the first day of winter, it must have been cold. Juan Diego had been waiting close to five hours, patiently sitting. One can understand why he kept his hat on. His tilma, hardly a warm piece of clothing, was wrapping the precious flowers. Most likely, he was wearing only his loincloth and sandals. The poor man must have been freezing after walking in the cold early morning for three to four hours and then sitting five hours in the same place. His meekness is truly moving. One can understand why the venerable Bishop broke into tears, profusely asking Juan Diego to forgive him for having allowed his servants to mistreat St Mary's ambassador.

The scene confirms the words of Our Lady: "I will honor you." Our humble hero is left standing before a number of important people kneeling before him, and he's wearing a hat, like a king, or a man of high nobility, indeed the highest nobility of them all: he belongs to the most exclusive club in the universe, he is the Ambassador of the Queen of Heaven, a saint of the Church advocating for his people before the Throne of God.

The Great Battle

Our Lady of Guadalupe appeared to Juan Diego at a momentous time in history. What we now call the Modern Age was starting, and the enemies of God had been gradually gaining ground since 1054 when the bishops of Rome and Constantinople exchanged excommunications thus dividing the Church into East and West. Now there were two new enemies: Islam, a movement that had appeared in the Arabian Peninsula during the 7th century; and the Enlightenment, a secular anti-clerical intellectual movement seeking to dislodge Western culture from Christianity. The Enlightenment was one of the unforeseen consequences of the German Reformation that began with Martin Luther in 1517. Their stories are related but it would take a whole new book to explain their relationship. We will only take a quick look at their origins here to get some idea of the challenges that Christendom was facing during that age.

By the mid 1400s, the troops of the Turkish Sultan were menacingly approaching Constantinople. They did not stop until they were defeated at the gates of Vienna. "The failure of the first [siege of Vienna] brought to a standstill the tide of Ottoman conquest which had been flooding up the Danube Valley for a century past."[121] As the Muslims pressed forward, many Oriental Christians escaped Asia Minor to seek refuge in Catholic Europe, bringing with them an anti-Roman attitude. That attitude, a distant echo of the Schism of 1054, was spread through Europe by those fleeing the Ottoman invasion in the East. Those seeds produced their fruit less than seven decades after the fall of Constantinople to the Turks. On October 31, 1517, Martin Luther presented his ninety theses in Wittenberg thus initiating the Western Schism.

Those who have in mind the words of St Paul in 2 Thessalonians 2:1-4 may begin to see the shape of that evil force—"the man of lawlessness"— becoming manifest at the beginning of the Modern Age: "As to the coming of our Lord Jesus Christ and our being gathered together to him, we beg you,

---

[121] Arnold Toynbee, *A Study of History*; Oxford University Press. p. 119.

brothers and sisters, not to be quickly shaken in mind or alarmed, either by spirit or by word or by letter, as though from us, to the effect that the day of the Lord is already here. Let no one deceive you in any way; for that day will not come unless the rebellion comes first and the man of lawlessness[122] is revealed, the one destined for destruction. He opposes and exalts himself above every so-called god or object of worship, so that he takes his seat in the temple of God, declaring himself to be God."

It is remarkable that both the German Reformation and Mohammedanism had in common their antipathy towards Rome. Even more remarkable is their negation of spiritual paternity. Muslims do not believe that Almighty God is a Father. Their concept of God is different and they reject the Christian understanding of the paternity of God. The German Reformers never rejected that traditional concept but they ceased to recognize the Roman Vicar of Christ as a spiritual father. That dangerous negation had fatal consequences because it created a dangerous political and cultural climate that made possible a number of future rebellions. The French Revolutionaries successfully revolted against their King, inaugurating an era of instability that continues to this day, the era of Socialism, Fascism, Communism, Anarchism, and the *Kulturkampf,* the cultural struggle that we still endure. All those forces have one common enemy, the Catholic Church. The rebellion appears in history as a violent flood very similar in nature to the malignant river that issues from the mouth of the dragon described in Revelation 12: "And when the dragon saw that he was cast unto the earth, he persecuted the woman, who brought forth the man child: And there were given to the woman two wings of a great eagle, that she might fly into the desert unto her place, where she is nourished for a time and times, and half a time, away from the face of the serpent. And the serpent cast out of his mouth after the woman, water as it were a river; that he might cause her to be carried away by the river."[123]

On 29 May, 1453, Constantinople was finally conquered by the Ottomans. That was an awful defeat for Christendom. Tasting the bitter fruits of division did not move the European side of Christendom to unite. The Sultan made Constantinople his new capital, renaming it Istanbul. Thus fell the city where the image carved by St Luke was first honored. Constantinople had lasted 499 years separated from the See of Peter. The Christians in the East were to suffer both Muslim and Communist oppression for many centuries to come.

The Ottomans, encouraged by their victory over the Christian forces, began to prepare for the final assault on Europe by building the largest Mediterranean fleet ever. In spite of the obvious danger, the Europeans remained divided.

Pope Pius V and many other alert Christians could see the Ottoman

---

[122] Man of sin, ο άνθρωπος της αμαρτίας, ο *ánthropos tis amartías.*
[123] Revelation 12:13-15.

power building up. They knew Italy was going to be their first target. Spain was devastated by centuries of Muslim domination. They could only be dislodged after many years of wars that had left Spain almost in ruins. The Pope did not want that for Italy. If Italy fell under Muslim power, he knew that was going to be the beginning of the end for Christian Europe. Pope Pius appealed to Phillip II. France, Germany, England, and the Netherlands remained on the sidelines. The pressure of St Pius V—one of the greatest Popes ever—moved Spain and Venice to participate. In the end Spain, Venice, Genoa, Sicily, the little island of Malta, and the Papal States had to face the invaders. The Christian fleet was under the command of Don John of Austria, the bastard son of Charles V and dearest half-brother of King Phillip of Spain. King Phillip had received a copy of the Miraculous Tilma from Don Montufar, Archbishop of Mexico. Before the battle, he gave the image of Our Lady to Admiral Giovanni Andrea Doria, commander of the Genovese fleet.

The two armadas met before sunrise early in the morning of October 7, 1571. In Rome, Pope Pius V urged all of Europe to pray the Holy Rosary asking for the victory of the Christian League. The Turks had the most powerful fleet ever to sail the Mediterranean. Among the rowers in the Turkish fleet there were thousands of Christian slaves. The European fleet was smaller but they had the greatest weapon: they were men of faith, true soldiers of Christ.

The wind did not favor the Christians but Christians all over Europe were praying the Holy Rosary for them. Don John raised the Papal Standard thus giving the signal to attack. The Turks, with the wind on their sails took only a short time to approach the Christian fleet. At that point something completely unusual happened: the wind stopped for a short time and started blowing in the opposite direction. The Christians, now with the wind on their side began a ferocious artillery attack. The change of wind had basically placed the Ottomans within the range of Christian artillery. The resulting smoke floated towards the enemy, blinding them. After the battle, many of the liberated Christian rowers told Don John that they had seen angels and saints, with swords drawn blowing clouds of smoke on the enemy's fleet.

It was a long and terrible battle that lasted from the first light of morning until night. Pope Pius V prayed all day. After a procession to the church of Santa Maria sopra Minerva, he was conversing with some Cardinals present there when suddenly, he stood looking up to the sky for a few minutes. Returning from that brief vision he informed the Cardinals: "This is not the moment to talk. We must give thanks for the victory God has granted to the Christian arms." Angels had brought to him the news of the victory at Lepanto. The event was documented and officially attested. Later on, those documents were entered into the canonization process of St Pius V.

Our Lady of Guadalupe received her baptism of fire at Lepanto. Her figure standing on the crescent moon—the main symbol of Islam—showed the world that she was a warrior Queen and Mother. The replica of the Miraculous Tilma held by Admiral Doria during that battle remained with the Doria family for many years until 1811, when it was finally donated by one of the descendants of the Admiral, Cardinal Giovanni Doria Pamphili, to the church of Santo Stefano d'Aveto, in the Liguria region of Italy.

In the centuries to come, the humble tilma of Juan Diego Cuauhtlatoatzin, the Speaking Eagle of Tepeyac, was going to be present in many conflicts, always on the side of Christ, life, and freedom.

8
A RIVER OF LIGHT

We have seen how Our Lady of Guadalupe presented the Church with a living *amoxtli*, a codex given to the people through St Juan Diego. We have seen also how that resulted in the conversion of millions of Mexicans to the faith of Christ. Even to this day, the Miraculous Tilma continues to silently convert souls with Mary's message of hope. We have seen how the image of Our Lady of Guadalupe delivers a Christian message using the complex iconography of the Aztec religion, playing a counterpoint of sorts between Coatlicue, their mother of the gods, and the "perfect Virgin Mary Mother of God Our Queen"—to use the words of Antonio Valeriano in the Nican Mopohua. This is not the first time that counterpoints are used to teach great truths. In fact, Holy Scripture is filled with lessons that make good use of that method. We are going to review one that is quite important to understanding the role of Mary of Nazareth in the salvation of mankind.

This is what we read in the Book of Genesis about Eve, the mother of mankind: "The serpent was the most clever of all the wild animals that God had created. The serpent said to the woman: 'Has God told you not to eat from any tree in the Garden?' And the woman responded: 'We are allowed to eat the fruit from any tree in the Garden but from the fruit of the tree that is in the middle of the Garden, God has told us not to eat from it, neither touch it lest we shall die.' Then the serpent said to the woman: 'No, you shall not die. God knows very well that when you eat from that tree, your eyes shall be opened and you shall be like God, knowing good and evil.' *Then the woman saw that the fruit of the tree was good to eat, a delight to behold, and she desired to acquire wisdom*; she took the fruit and ate some of it, and later she gave it to her husband who was with her, and he also ate."[124]

That is the sad story of Eve, the first woman. She was deceived into joining the devil's rebellion against God's sovereign paternity. Sin and death entered the world as a result of Eve's disobedience. Eve became the mother of a condemned race.

From that moment, God began to work to rescue mankind. In the fullness

---

[124] Genesis 3:1-6.

of time, God sent his Son to be born of a woman named Mary of Nazareth.

Here we find our first counterpoint: just as Eve had accepted the proposal of a bad angel—who presented himself as a serpent—Mary accepted the mission that God communicated to her through a holy angel:

"In the sixth month, the angel Gabriel was sent by God to a town in Galilee called Nazareth, to a virgin betrothed to a man called Joseph, of the house of David. The virgin's name was Mary, and [the angel] came to her and said, 'Hail, full of grace, the Lord is with you: blessed are you among women.' But she was troubled by his words and pondered what manner of greeting this might be. The angel said to her, 'Do not be afraid, Mary, for you have found grace with God. Behold, you will conceive in your womb and bear a son, and you shall name him Jesus. He will be great, and will be called the Son of the Most High, and the Lord God will give to him the throne of David his father. He will reign over the house of Jacob forever, and his kingdom will have no end.' Mary said to the angel, 'How can this be since I know no man?' The angel said to her, 'The Holy Spirit will come upon you, and the power of the Most High will overshadow you; therefore the child to be born will be holy; he will be called Son of God. [...] And Mary said: 'Behold the handmaid of the Lord; let it be done to me according to thy word.' Then the angel departed from her."[125]

By being disobedient, Eve gave birth to a race condemned to sin and death. By being obedient, Mary gave birth to Jesus, who was born to liberate mankind from sin and death. Through Mary, God is undoing the error of Eve. Through Jesus, God is undoing the sin of Adam.

Counterpoints

Deceived by the serpent, Eve began to look at the fruit of the forbidden tree as something desirable. Her husband had taught her about that prohibition and the consequences of violating it. In fact, everything that Eve knew about the Garden, and life, she had learned from Adam. The serpent cleverly planted in Eve's mind the possibility of having some knowledge of her own. Perhaps she thought that having the wisdom of God would be something great, particularly if there was no punishment for disobeying the commandment.[126] That desire grew in Eve's mind fueled by her newly discovered hunger to get some of God's wisdom. By the time she took the first bite, she had implicitly called God a liar but God was not lying. The moment she disobeyed, she began to die. Inside her, all of humankind began to die also. In a few years, envy caused the death of one of her children. In

---

[125] Luke 2:26-38.

[126] One of the latest slogans used by those who seek to introduce heterodox practices into the Catholic Church is: "God does not punish". After so many centuries, the methods of temptation have not changed that much.

fact, the sin of envy had infected the whole human race through Eve.

When Mary of Nazareth received the angel and learned that she was going to be the mother of the Messiah, she obediently accepted her mission without hesitation. With perfect humility, she consented to be the instrument of God for the sanctification of the world. From that very moment, she declared her belief in the truthfulness of God. In that instant, the world began imperceptibly to return to God's perfect order. And yet, Mary did not know that she was going to lead the fight for the liberation of all mankind.

Several decades later, Mary was at Calvary, standing at the foot of the Cross. Since the day when Jesus was presented to St Simeon at the Temple in Jerusalem, she had lived in dread of that terrible moment. The Church failed at that first horrific crisis: Peter, the leader of Christ's apostles, denied him three times and fled. Judas committed suicide. The other nine apostles went into hiding. Only John remained next to Mary. Her physical and spiritual perfection only helped to make her pain grow more acute. The view of the brutalized body of her Son pierced her heart like a thousand arrows. Within her, the pain grew unabated. The years of murmurs and shame at her untimely pregnancy, the accusations of the Pharisees, and the ungratefulness of her own people were nothing compared to the sight of Jesus crucified. At one point, her motherly heart desired so strongly to be crucified in his place. So many times he had told his disciples that it was necessary for him to suffer but no one quite understood the meaning of his words. Now she wanted trade places with him with every fiber of her body, she wanted the Cross all for herself. If she had been God at that very moment, she would have exchanged places with her Son, but she was not God, she was just Mary, the carpenter's widow contemplating how the Roman Empire, and the religious leaders of Israel, were killing her only Son. He, that once rested safely in the crossing of her arms.[127]

In the darkness of that unspeakable pain, Mary alone, little Mary of Nazareth undid the snare of the serpent and rescued humankind from the consequences of Eve's envy. The fate of the entire universe came to bear on Mary's heart. She was Christ's helper[128] and she proved to be up to the task. Alone and bereft of any help, she discovered the wisdom of the Cross, she understood the prophecy of Simeon—"And thy own soul a sword shall

---

[127] "When our Lord announced to His Blessed Mother what was going to take place, She besought Him, in the most touching terms, to let Her die with Him. ....She did not weep much, but her grief was indescribable, and there was something almost awful in Her look of deep recollection. Our Divine Lord returned thanks, as a loving Son, for all the love She had borne Him, and pressed Her to His heart." *The Dolorous Passion of Our Lord Jesus Christ. Meditation V*, by Blessed Anne Catherine Emmerich.

[128] Genesis 2:18 – "And the Lord God said: It is not good for man to be alone: let us make for him a helper."

pierce"—and she did what no one in the whole world could do as she could—she desired the Cross with perfect intensity, and in doing so, she obtained a measure of the wisdom of God that was commensurate with her title of *Kecharitomene*.[129] The One Full of Grace was now also filled with divine sapience. The curse of the serpent was broken and Mary entered history working with her Son to liberate the world.[130]

The Perfect Mother

How difficult it is to write about holy perfection with an imperfect heart! Our Lady of Guadalupe introduced herself as the "Perfect Virgin Holy Mary, Mother of God" because she had the right to announce her perfection, and to make it a model for the new nation whose birth she was bringing to fruition. As a Jewess she had heard the Law: "You shall be holy, for I the LORD your God am holy. You shall honor your mother and father, and you keep my Sabbaths holy: I am the LORD your God [...] You shall not hate your brother in your heart; you shall admonish your neighbor, or you will be guilty yourself. You shall not take vengeance or bear a grudge against any of your brethren, but you shall love your neighbor as yourself. I am the LORD."[131]

She was also in perfect compliance with her Son's commandment: "You must therefore be perfect as your heavenly Father is perfect."[132] Her wisdom and perfection were given to her because of the merits of her Son when she generously surrendered herself completely to the will of God in an act of supreme confidence and trust. Hers was truly the wisdom of the Cross expounded by St Paul: "... If you think that you are wise in this age, you should become fools so that you may become wise. For the wisdom of this world is foolishness with God."[133]

Mary could call herself perfect because she was ready to comply with something that—for ordinary persons—is an impossible demand, something exceeding the capabilities of human nature. Her Son demanded a radical change in the very nature of his followers and gave the example on the Cross, dying and asking God to forgive those responsible for murdering him. When he had almost accomplished his sacrifice, Jesus gave us Mary as a perfect example for the faithful Church, and also gave the Church to Mary: "When Jesus saw his mother and the beloved disciple standing next to her, he said to his mother, 'Woman, here is your son.' Then he said to the disciple, 'Here is your mother.'"[134] John, the beloved disciple was the only Apostle standing

---

[129] "Full of grace". *Gr.* Κεχαριτωμένης.

[130] Psalm 110 (109):1-2 — The LORD says to my lord, 'Sit at my right hand until I make your enemies your footstool.' The Lord sends out from Zion your mighty scepter. Rule in the midst of your foes.

[131] Leviticus 19:1-3; 17-18.

[132] Matthew 5: 33-48.

[133] See 1 Corinthians 3:16-20.

next to the Cross and next to Mary. He is an enduring example of faithfulness for all bishops and all disciples through the ages.

Neither John nor Mary refused to work with Peter or with any of the other nine Apostles. They did not start a new "denomination" but humbly submitted to the authority of those whom Jesus had designated as Apostles in spite of their imperfections. When Our Lady of Guadalupe appeared to Gil Cordero in Extremadura, she sent him with a message to the authorities of the Church. She did the exact same thing with Juan Diego on Tepeyac Hill. The wisdom of the Cross requires obedience, even when a Pope does awful things, like denying the Lord, or acting cowardly in the face of danger.

When Mary—acting even against her instinct of self-preservation—*desired* for herself the agony of her Son, she was undoing the error of Eve. But unlike Eve's, her sons and daughters were not in her physical womb, they were already born in the flesh and spread all over the world. She had to participate with Christ and the faithful Church to give them everlasting life. The many apparitions of Our Lady throughout time are proof of her loving interest and participation in the work of redeeming the world.

The Grand Parable

We find the Song of Mary, the *Magnificat*, in the Gospel of Luke. Extolling the power and mercy of God, Our Lady says: "His mercy is for those who fear him from generation to generation. He has shown strength with his arm; He has scattered the proud in the thoughts of their hearts. He has brought down the powerful from their thrones, and lifted up the lowly." It was A.D. 357 when the relics of St Luke were taken to Constantinople. The long centuries of persecutions were coming to an end, and Christianity was advancing in vanquishing the proud gods of the Roman Empire when the image carved by St Luke appeared on the world scene.[135] She had a scepter in her right hand, and the Holy Child on her left arm. Emperor Flavius Julius Constantius Augustus received her with great honors and a royal procession accompanied the image to the Cathedral. She was still there when the New Cathedral was built by Emperor Justinian I circa A.D. 532. It was named the Church of the Holy Wisdom[136] in honor of the Logos, the Second Person of the Holy Trinity. In A.D. 582, Emperor Mauritius married Constantina, the daughter of Emperor Tiberius. On August 13 of that year, he succeeded his father-in-law as Emperor. He was the one who gave the precious relic to St Gregory, who

---

[134] John 19:26-27.

[135] The image carved by St Luke emerged from burial twice, in Greece first and later, in Spain. That calls to mind the Resurrection, the promise of a new life taught in the Gospels. Both visions of Our Lady of Guadalupe, in Spain and Mexico, are strongly life-affirming.

[136] Ναὸς τῆς Αγίας τοῦ Θεού Σοφίας, *Naos tēs Hagias tou Theou Sophias*, Temple of the Holy Wisdom of God.

was the Papal Ambassador to the imperial court. Gregory was the one who brought the image of Our Lady to Rome. Soon after, Gregory was elected Pope. He is the Pope we now know as Gregory the Great. The miraculous image, a veritable treasure of grace, was then given to St Isidore of Seville in A.D. 595, perhaps because Rome was always in danger of being raided by the Lombards and Seville was a more secure place to keep it. The relic was sent as a present to Isidore's brother, St Leander who was at that time the Bishop of Seville. That is how the image made it to Spain.

From the vantage point of our age, we can see how the image that one day was going to be Our Lady of Guadalupe traveled many centuries—from A.D. 359 to A.D. 595—across the decaying Roman Empire that was being dismembered by various invaders in fulfillment of St John's prophecy: "After this I saw another angel coming down from heaven, having great authority; and the earth was made bright with his splendor. He called out with a mighty voice, 'Fallen, fallen is Babylon the great!'"[137] The angel calls Rome "Babylon the great" because both mighty Rome and ancient Babylon destroyed Jerusalem at different times. A fateful coincidence united both destructions of the Temple of Jerusalem: in 587 B.C., the Babylonians had breached the walls on the 17th day of the Hebrew month of Tamuz, reaching and destroying the Temple on the 9th day of Av. Nine centuries later in A.D. 70, the legions of Roman general Titus Vespasian breached the walls and destroyed the Temple on the same dates, thus fulfilling the prophecy written in Matthew 24: "As Jesus came out of the Temple, and as he was going away, his disciples showed him the Temple buildings. Then he asked them: 'Do you see all these things? Verily I tell you, not one stone will be left here upon another that will not be thrown down.'"[138] The time had come for the Romans to taste the bitter fruits of destruction that they so generously had served to so many peoples and nations. Strangely enough, the barbarians that brought Rome to her knees were later converted by the Church; they were the seed of the future Christendom. In my view, that is no mere coincidence. That was part of the grand parable built around that small image that emerged from St Luke's grave to travel all the way to Tenochtitlan. Innumerable miracles happened as she moved through space and time: nations were liberated, pestilence was halted, battles were won, empires were established, wicked oppression ended, enemies of Christ were vanquished, and millions of souls were converted. When we observe the whole path, from the first century to our present, we can see a distinct pattern of liberation. The message is clear, Mary is preparing the way for the second arrival of her Son. In essence, her actions are saying to believers in every age: "Am I not here, I who am your mother?" We can see God guiding history through Mary. She prepared a place for Christ to arrive

---

[137] Revelation 18:1-24.
[138] Matthew 24:1-2.

the first time; she is doing the same now. She will have the world ready for the advent of her Son. Those who look at history with the eyes of faith can see her work in every generation.

The City of God

From the African side of the Mediterranean, St Augustine of Hippo[139] looked at Rome as the mother of civilization, the keeper of the Pax Romana, the Roman Law, the arts, and also of that new strength that had appeared in Palestine three centuries before, Christianity, a force that was giving the old empire a new impulse—not to conquer nations to bring them into the Roman order but to evangelize them, bringing them into Christ's flock. That vision of Augustine was shattered when the news of the sack of Rome by the Vandals arrived in 410 A.D.

It must have been a terrible shock for a Bishop like him. The same man that converted to Christianity in 387 when no one could even imagine that barbarians would one day humiliate Rome. Augustine himself represented the fusion of two worlds that met in his own soul. Pagan Augustine was immersed in the classic Greco-Roman culture. When he decided to become a Christian, his powerful intellect struggled to find a way to combine the best of his world with this new Christian order filled with promise and hope.

When Rome fell, Augustine's conception of the world fell with her. He went into the depths of his soul, seeking a way to reconcile the reality of the perishing Roman order with the chrysalis of Christendom emerging from the ruins. That new order began to emerge in his thoughts and the thoughts of the Fathers of the Church that followed him, those who began to shape Christian Europe into what we now call Western Civilization. From the dark night of Rome's demise, many Christian cultures were going to grow under the sign of the Cross, but the Christian West was still too far in the future for Augustine to see.

Augustine realized that it was not possible to reconcile the reality of history within the narrow limits of philosophy. Our saint had to re-evaluate history with the help of God's grace. We can trace a significant part of the theological science of the Church to that Augustinian reflection. Many centuries were to pass before the powerful intellect of Thomas Aquinas would elevate Christian thought to new heights.

Augustine had to contemplate "in one hour"—to use the words of St. John—the collapse of a civilization that considered itself "the world" and claimed the whole Mediterranean as "our sea." The enormous magnitude of

---

[139] St. Augustine of Hippo was born on November 13, A.D. 354 and died on August 28, A.D. 430. He is a Doctor of the Church, and one of the Early Fathers, a philosopher and the first to make an attempt at developing a systematic theology. He was the bishop of Hippo Regius in what is now Tunisia, North Africa.

that debacle cannot be compared to the slow but sure decline of the Western Civilization we grew up in. We have seen decades go by, each one leaving its own record of decay. Augustine had only one short and brutal report arriving perhaps with a ship that managed to escape: "Rome was sacked by the Vandals." I dare to guess that he did not miss the irony of being so close to Carthage, erased from the face of the Earth by Scipio as just punishment for her horrible sins. Now it was Rome's time to pay.

Augustine had to understand that terrible new reality and struggle to re-interpret the very meaning of human history, of which Rome was the most complete and perfect expression. It is good to keep in mind that what we call today "our civilization" has been around for quite a shorter time than the Greco-Roman world which itself was a magnificent triumph of mankind barely emerging from the rough life of prehistoric Europe. Politics, philosophy, engineering, arts, sciences ... everything was the product of that long twilight of Greek paganism that later found new impetus in the strength of Rome. The world was filled with marvelous things never before seen. But in the three decades since the conversion of Augustine, the world had passed from total order to almost total breakdown. That hit Augustine with such force that he was moved to think that perhaps there was something in the violence and stupidity of the pagan past that had started the destruction of the world a long time before he was born. What Augustine did not see—because he was too close to the scene—was that the empty husk of the Roman Empire had to break and fall to give way to the new Christian reality. The Church was ready for those "bigger things"[140] that Christ had talked about less than four centuries before.

Augustine found himself in a new reality and suddenly realized that his intellectual toolbox was equipped to deal with it. There was no way to understand the sudden fall of Rome in a strictly historical setting. I am sure he thought of the "little apocalypse" found in Matthew chapter 24. The Fathers of the Church saw in that prediction of the end of unfaithful Jerusalem a scale model of the final days of the world. Our saint had to make use of theology; he had to distance himself from material reality and see things from the perspective of Heaven. Leaving behind the city that men were building, he got closer to the city of God being built mysteriously in Heaven with bricks hardened in the fires of the world. In that burning world, Augustine woke up to the eternal realities that he had imperfectly seen before. Now the domes of the celestial city were shining before his eyes. In the light of Rome's great fire, Augustine the African could see the Heavenly Jerusalem for the first time. That is the genesis of *De Civitate Dei*. That is how Augustine got the idea that

---

[140] John 14:12 – "In truth I tell you, he who believes in me will also do the works that I do and moreover, will do even greater works, because I am going to the Father."

those two cities are part of the plan of God for mankind.

The sacking of Rome brought about the birth of Christendom and in due time, the conversion of the descendants of those barbarians who had sacked Rome.

What intellectuals lack today is the theological vision of history that Augustine used to comprehend the ultimate reality. That missing element is what modern intellectuals need to understand the disaster unfolding before their very eyes. Alas, for them it is no longer licit to understand history in theological terms. Even when Marxism's "scientific" understanding of history has failed catastrophically, very few have taken notice. Men—to quote St. John again—"repented not from their sins"[141] to the point of refusing to acknowledge the imminent demise of the perverse system they have created. Just as Christendom was a new morning for Rome, there is a new dawn coming for this world. Christ has not revealed yet the name of that age but we know it will come because he said: "Heaven and earth will pass away, but my words will never pass away" (Matthew 24:35). Like Augustine, we cannot see it yet but we can hope for it in our hearts, knowing that it won't fail to arrive.

The humble image carved by St Luke in the first century was a silent witness of all those cosmic upheavals. Looking at all those events from a distance of centuries it is possible to discern a pattern: the oppressively legalistic religious system of Judea that had condemned Jesus, had to come to an end. The Roman Empire that St John called "Babylon the Great" was destroyed "in one hour." The long stay of the Muslim occupiers of Spain ended after centuries of violent struggle. The Aztec system of oppression and terror also ended abruptly with the arrival of Cortez.

Using St Augustine's perspective, we can see that all those things were replaced by something new. The Jewish religious system, and the pagan religious order, gave way to Christianity and the Church. Rome was replaced by the Holy Roman Empire, and Christendom. The Muslim order in Spain was replaced by a new nation that turned into a vast empire almost overnight as new lands were discovered. From the ashes of the Triple Alliance, the Mexican nation was born with a new Christian identity. The victory at Lepanto prevented the Muslims from dominating the strategic Mediterranean Sea, thus preparing the way for the great economic expansion that followed when commercial routes were opened to the Orient and the Americas. In the end, Catholic Christianity extended to the most distant parts of the world.[142] The root of all those changes in the world can be traced back to Calvary. It

---

[141] Revelation 16:9 – "And men were scorched with great heat, and they blasphemed the name of God, who hath power over these plagues, neither did they penance to give him glory." *Douay-Rheims*.

[142] Mark 16:15-16 – "And [Jesus] said to them, 'Go into all the world and proclaim the Gospel to the whole creation. Those who believe and are baptized will be saved; but those who do not believe will be condemned."

was there that Christ and Mary defeated the original serpent and started to undo the damage done by the devil. That was only the beginning of a long battle to liberate the world. Liberation is at the center of that grand parable written in history. Every one of the events we have reviewed is a type, a model of a larger and final event. That is what the images of Our Lady of Guadalupe in Extremadura and Tepeyac are telling us.

The image of Our Lady revealed to Gil Cordero is a symbol of royal power. Our Lady has a scepter in one hand, and she is carrying the Divine Child. He is represented as a Child-King, his rule is just beginning[143] but the scepter is being held firmly by his Mother, the Queen. She is preparing the way for the King's Second Advent. The Prince of Peace is still a Child, symbolically speaking his time to reign is still in the future but he will grow to become a King. In his Mother's right hand is the "iron scepter" of justice that he will hold to rule the nations. From the grave of St Luke, that image advanced victoriously all the way to the altars of Moctezuma. The second image, given to St Juan Diego at Tepeyac Hill, traveled all the way to Lepanto, and then with the Church to the most distant corners of the world.

The image has also traveled in time to our days. The human figures reflected in her eyes could not be discovered with 16th century technology. No one in Mexico or Spain could yet go back in time and see that the positions of the stars in her mantle reflected the night sky over Mexico on December 12, 1531. The knowledge to make those complex astronomical calculations was still far in the future. Those messages are for us who have the science, the optical instruments, and the computers to see and understand what no ordinary person of that age could. For us in the 21st Century, the image has a slightly different message because the struggle against the forces of darkness has changed.

Our Lady of Guadalupe appeared to St Juan Diego only ten years after the conquest of Mexico by Cortez on the day of the Immaculate Conception. At that time, the Spaniards did not completely control their vast new domains in America. That allowed the horrible human sacrifices to continue for a while in particular, infant sacrifices. When Our Lady of Guadalupe appeared, her perfect message reached places where the Spanish authorities did not have any influence at all: the conscience of the natives. "I am truly your merciful mother, the mother of all the people of this land, and of all kinds of men who love me, who call for my help, seek me, and trust me. In that holy house, I will listen to their cries and sorrows, cure them of their many sufferings, miseries, and woes." Her message was as powerful as it was subtle. The light of the Christian truth illuminated the native conscience with a force that no set of human laws could carry. Our situation today is very similar: legal abortion, euthanasia, and many other evils are no longer crimes. Wicked

---

[143] See Psalm 110 (109):1-2.

ideologues working together with indifferent or corrupt politicians have made those abominations legal. In some parts of the world, abortion and self-induced suicide are considered human rights. As these lines are written, widespread infanticide is not very far in the future. Our young are also lost in many other ways: drug abuse, perverted sex, prostitution, pornography, etc. Those practices are destroying not only individual lives but the life and culture of the societies that tolerate and promote them.

It is nearly impossible to figure the exact number of people who were sacrificed by the predecessors and followers of Tlecaellel. It would be still harder if we attempted to estimate the number of human sacrifices perpetrated before the discovery. The truth is that the arrival of the Europeans in America did not put an end to exterminations or oppression. Many saints such as Bishop Zumárraga or San Francisco Solano, preached against the unfair practices to which some natives were subjected in the past five centuries.

In recent years, one could affirm there has been a resurgence of ideas and practices so bloody, cruel, and demonic as those of Tlecaellel—and even more vicious. Just below the surface of our modern culture lies an invisible but heartbreaking world of human suffering and violence. Pro-abortion organizations have managed to alter the legal traditions and laws of many countries and in such places as the United States, tens of millions of legal abortions have been performed so far. Unfortunately, legal abortion was only the beginning of a series of abominations, some of which are inconceivably inhuman and satanic.

One cannot help asking in earnest: what is God going to do to stop this new generation of murderers? Truly, the infamous record of Tlecaellel and his cronies has been more than exceeded. It should not come as a surprise if the divine punishment for such crimes is greater than that received by our pre-Columbian forefathers. This is a sobering thought that should motivate faithful Catholics to evangelize the New World once again. Evangelization is—as it always has been—not a matter of choice but a matter of life and death both for nations and individuals. It is up to us to choose life for the world before we run out of time.

EPILOGUE

When Bishop Zumarraga was sent to Mexico with both spiritual and temporal powers, he had authority to act in the name of God and Crown. At the time of the miracle, the Crown of Spain was resting on one of the most Catholic heads ever to hold the title of King: Charles V, the grandson of Queen Isabella and King Ferdinand, a Habsburg, and a faithful Catholic monarch if there was ever one. Understandably, he was a contemporary of St John of the Cross, and St Teresa of Avila, among other Spanish saints. King Charles was also the father of Don John of Austria, the victor of Lepanto.

Bishop Zumarraga was chosen to represent such a noble and gracious monarch. He was sent to defend the native Mexicans from a group of rapacious Spaniards who opposed the conversion of his new Mexican subjects. At the same time, there were some natives who did not want any Mexicans to convert to the faith of the conquerors, and some decent Spaniards who opposed their avaricious compatriots. To sum up the situation, everyone was fighting everyone. Bishop Zumarraga was a man of strong faith and he did what a man of faith does when facing a desperate situation: he fell to his knees and poured prayer after prayer before the Lord. On December 8, 1531, he spent the day in prayer. In a secret report sent to King Charles, he had written his now famous words: "Unless there is supernatural intervention, the country is lost."

The answer to his prayers did not tarry long. Our Lady of Guadalupe appeared to St Juan Diego at daybreak the following day. Three and a half days later, Juan Diego was pouring roses before the astonished Bishop, and the story of the Miraculous Tilma began. Three and a half days, the same length of time of the Passion. It took thirteen days to build the first chapel at the Cerrito, Tepeyac Hill. Only one day after Christmas the conversions began: nine million natives were baptized. A Catholic nation was born of Mary in a near instant. "Who has ever heard such a thing? and who has seen the like of it? shall the earth bring forth in one day? or shall a nation be born at once, because Zion has been in labor, and has brought forth her children?"[144]

In the days of our first mother, Eve, the world was lost to sin. Eve was

---

[144] Isaiah 66: 8.

tempted to envy the knowledge of God. She could not understand her destiny, the honor of being the physical and spiritual mother of all humanity, because she was deceived, desiring for herself the knowledge that God had justly reserved for Himself. Eve was tempted to envy the wisdom of God.

"But the serpent answered the woman thus: 'It is not true that you are going to die, God knows very well that, when you eat from the fruit of that tree, your eyes will be opened and you will become like God, knowing good and evil.' Then the woman saw that the fruit of the tree was good for eating, that it looked good to eat, and she desired for herself the wisdom that it could give her, so she took it and ate. And then she gave some to her husband, who also ate." [145]

After the fall, Adam gave his wife the name of "Mother" (in Hebrew, *Ava*). "The man called his wife Eve because she was going to be the mother of everyone who lived." [146]

Unfortunately for us, when Eve was seduced by the devil's lies, our first mother had all the unborn humans in her womb. As a result, all humanity inherited sin and death. That woman, destined to be the mother of humanity, chose to give birth to a condemned race. One could consider that terrible mistake as a first and massive abortion. Interestingly, our word "abortion" comes from two Latin words, *ab* (outside, ripped out) and *hortus / ortus* (garden / birth) 'what is outside the garden' or 'what does not bloom'. Adam and Eve were justly judged for their disobedience and were thrown out of the Garden of Eden carrying all their descendants in tow.

The race condemned to death by the envy of one mother had to be rescued by the generous gift of another Mother, Mary of Nazareth. Just as Eve in the Garden of Eden coveted the fruit of the tree (*Gr.* xylon) and brought upon herself and her husband the judgment of God; the night before the Crucifixion, the Son of Mary had been arrested and violently taken out of the Garden of Gethsemane to face an unjust and unmerciful trial. Once at Calvary, Mary of Nazareth desired for herself the fruit of a much less desirable tree, the Cross (*Gr.* xylon, stavros) because in her pure and immaculate heart, our perfect mother desired for herself the pains of the Cross and wished to suffer in place of her Son. There we find a revelation: that therefore the fruit of the Cross must be equal to the wisdom of God to perfectly compensate the error that led Adam and Eve to original sin. What a profound mystery we have before us!

Juan Diego judged it well when, listening to the song of the birds in the Tepeyac, he thought that he had wandered into paradise, the original garden of his ancestors. Through that humble macehual, Mary was going to invite the Mexican people to the delights of heavenly life. Those who one day were

---

[145] Genesis 3:4-6.
[146] Genesis 3:20.

deceived and walked away from God and salvation, were now invited to retrace their steps, following Mary who would lead them to Jesus and salvation. That meant entering with her into battle against evil. The Mexican eagle was now going to fight alongside Our Lady of Guadalupe against the original serpent.

Throughout history, the enemy of God has been preparing for the final battle. He knows he is going to lose but his will is fixed on rebellion. He cannot repent or surrender. When the final battle comes, the enemy wants to have all the troops he can gather. The most rebellious of his fallen angels have been prisoners in deep wells of darkness since the days of Noah's Flood.[147] As the day of battle approaches, the devil must set them free. In a grotesque mockery of God's redemptive love, he has recruited many human mothers to offer the innocent blood of their unborn children to help the cause of the demons. The devil has cajoled and connived millions of mothers into the practice of abortion. A few of those mothers know perfectly well what they're doing but most of them continue to be fooled just like Eve was.

In our days, the demonic forces have many human allies. The devil has blinded the leaders of mankind into making rapid changes to social structures built with the experience of millennia. As a result, societies across the globe are becoming brittle. The continuous assault of Cultural Marxism has redefined the role of men, women, children, education, sexual mores, etc. all at once without any regard to consequences. One among many undesirable results of birth control and legal abortion is quite evident among those living in the so-called developed countries: while birth rates drop, immigration grows. Europeans are importing population from Africa and the Middle East to replace their own young ones that will never be born. Americans are likewise importing young Latin Americans. This is simply a huge population replacement operation. The present generations are giving away the future to have a better life today at any cost. Can you see the parallel with Eve, who sacrificed everything she had by taking what amounted to a suicidal shortcut?

The West is now at a crossroads. All those evil actions have caused too much discontent. Some of the Spanish conquerors of Mexico thought it was easy to defeat and enslave a group of savages to enrich themselves quickly. The result was a societal collapse so fast that it could have resulted in the total loss of the Mexican nation. Thank God for one faithful Bishop. That is all it took to solve the problem: one good heart, two knees, and prayer.

Much has been prophesied about the moral condition of the world before the Second Coming of Our Lord. We are told to expect an unprecedented and massive outbreak of evil that will spread chaos, sedition, revolution, war,

---

[147] St Jude 6 – "And the angels who did not keep their own position, but left their proper dwelling, [God] has kept in eternal chains in deepest darkness for the judgment of the great day."

and all manner of human suffering on a worldwide scale. We are told to expect apostasy and schism in the Church as darkness sets in upon the world and the devil deceives most of mankind to reject truth and accept his lies. Yet, we are told that a small remnant will not fall for that deception because they will be heeding the Lord's warning: "Gird yourselves and have your lamps burning; be like those who are waiting for their master to return from the wedding banquet, so that they may open the door to receive him as soon as he comes and knocks. Blessed are those servants whom the master finds *on the watch*..."[148]

The fall of Tenochtitlan and the conquest of Mexico can be used as an eschatological scale model. The Church was going through the pains of the Reformation, and the parallelism between the Aztec culture and today's Western culture are really hard to miss. The crisis in Mexico reached a point of no return, forcing Bishop Zumarraga to conclude that only a supernatural intervention could solve the dire situation. It may come to pass that we have to live through a replay of the fall of Tenochtitlan, this time on a global scale.

One day, the Church will pass through a final trial that will shake the faith of many. For those who are prepared, those trials will not come as a surprise. It happened to the early Church, and it was registered in the Gospels so that we learn the lesson and know how to act when our time comes. The day when Christ was crucified on Mount Calvary all his apostles—except one—deserted him, the first Pope denied him three times, and one of His bishops committed suicide. The one that faithfully stood by the Cross was the youngest, the one that only a few hours earlier had heard the soft and steady beating of the Sacred Heart while his head was resting on his Master's chest. That was John, the beloved disciple, the Son of Thunder, the Soaring Eagle. John's young soul was not prepared for the kind of darkness that descended on them after the Last Supper. Everyone around him failed, except Jesus' mother and yet he did not fail. He did not "form his own church" to separate from the others who had abandoned their Master. Later, after the Resurrection, John did not question the authority of Peter or any of the other Apostles.[149]

John was able to remain faithful to the bitter end because he was close to Mary. When darkness comes and even the Church and the Pope fail to reflect the light of Christ, we have to remember the example of John. Those who remain close to Mary will be given the strength to be faithful: "When Jesus therefore had seen his mother and the disciple whom he loved standing, he said to his mother: 'Woman, behold thy son.' After that, he said to the disciple: 'Behold thy mother.' And from that hour, the disciple took her to his

---

[148] Luke 12: 35-40.

[149] See John 20: 3-8 when John arrives first at the empty tomb. He does not enter first but respectfully waits for Peter to arrive.

own home."[150] On a different mountain, far away from Calvary both in time and space, Juan Diego Cuauhtlatoatzin, the Speaking Eagle, was given the same privilege, to have the Mother of Our Lord as his own mother when he heard these words from Our Lady of Guadalupe: "Am I not here? Am I not your Mother? Are you not under my shadow and protection? Am I not the source of your joy? Are you not in the hollow of my mantle, in the crossing of my arms?" Only after receiving that extraordinary personal grace, Juan Diego was given the miraculous image of Our Lady of Guadalupe. He also took her to his own home.

When the river issuing from the mouth of the dragon threatens to drown us all, when all that is firm and steady collapses all around us and we are standing alone before the Cross, we will take strength in Our Lady just like John, Juan Diego, the Christian fighters of Lepanto, and many others who had to face their own personal apocalypse. The river of impurity and death issuing from the devil is countered by this other river of light, not the literal Guadalupe River in Spain but the river of countless graces flowing from the blessed hands of Our Lady. She will generously dispense those graces and help us heal our world if we only ask her.

---

[150] John 19: 26-27.

TIMETABLE

84 – St Luke dies near Bœotia, Greece ca. A.D. 84

357 – Relics of St Luke are moved from Thebes to Constantinople.

430 – St Augustine of Hippo dies in Roman North Africa.

582 – St Gregory brings the image of Our Lady to Rome.

595 – St Isidore carries the image to Seville as a present to his brother St Leander.

636 – St Isidore dies in Seville.

410 – Sack of Rome by the Visigoths.

618 – Muhammad flees to Mecca; the era of Islamic expansion begins.

711 – Sevilian clergy flee north, carrying relics and the image carved by St Luke.
The Moors begin the Umayyad, the conquest of Roman Hispania.
Religious fleeing the Moorish invasion bury the image carved by St Luke near
the Guadalupe River in Extremadura, Spain.

712 – Roderic, last Visigoth king of Spain is killed battling the Moors.

722 – Pelayo, Pelagius of Asturias begins the Reconquest at Covadonga.

1212 – Spanish and Portuguese armies defeat the Moors at Las Navas de Tolosa.

1326 – The Virgin Mary appears to Gil Cordero, the relics are found.
Called Lady of Guadalupe for the first time.

1340 – Christian forces defeat the Moors at Rio Salado in Tarifa, Spain.

1398 – Birth of Tlecaellel, founder of the Aztec Empire.

1429 – The Triple Alliance, beginning of the Aztec Empire in Tenochtitlan.

1453 – Constantinople falls on May 29.

1468 – Don Juan de Zumarraga is born in Spain.

1474 – Juan Diego is born in Mexico, named Cuauhtlatouac.

1482 – Ferdinand of Castile takes control of Alhama. The War of Granada begins.

1487 – Tlecaellel inaugurates the Temple in Tenochtitlan, thousands are sacrificed.

1492 – End of the War of Granada. Columbus' expedition departs August 3.
Columbus arrives in Santo Domingo October 12.
Muslims expelled from Spain.

1510 – Diego de Velazquez settles in Cuba.

1517 – Martin Luther begins the German Reformation.

1519 – Hernan Cortez arrives in Mexico.

1521 – Aztec capital city Tenochtitlan falls.

1524 – Franciscan Friars arrive in Mexico.

1525 – Juan Diego Cuauhtlatouac is baptized.

1528 – Don Juan de Zumarraga arrives in Mexico.

1529 – Maria Lucia, wife of Juan Diego dies in Cuautitlan.

1531 – Halley's comet visible August 24.
    Pizarro sails to Peru from Panama.
    Our Lady of Guadalupe appears in Tepeyac.
1533 – Construction of the First Sanctuary.
1540 – Last expedition of Hernando De Soto lands in Florida.
1541 – Toribio de Benavente Motolinia reports nine million natives baptized.
1548 – Juan Diego Cuauhtlatoatzin and Fray Juan de Zumarraga die in Mexico.
1555 – Archbishop Montufar first approval of the apparitions.
1556 – Antonio Valeriano writes the *Nican Mopohua*.
1570 – An oil copy of the image is sent to King Philip II of Spain.
1571 – Battle of Lepanto.
    King Phillip II gives the copy of the image to Andrea Doria.
1597 – First English settlers reach the coast of Virginia.
1620 – English Puritans land in Plymouth, Massachusetts.
1649 – Lasso de la Vega publishes the *Nican Mopohua*.
1666 – Formal canonical investigation takes place.
1695 – New Sanctuary construction begins, dedicated in 1709.
1723 – Formal investigation ordered by Archbishop Lanziego y Eguilaz.
1737 – Our Lady of Guadalupe, Patroness of Mexico City.
1746 – Our Lady of Guadalupe, Patroness from California to El Salvador.
1746 – Boturini Benaducci promotes the solemn and official coronation of the image.
1754 – Pope Benedict XIV approves and sanctions a Mass and Office.
1756 – Miguel de Cabrera publishes his book *American Marvel*.
1757 – Our Lady of Guadalupe, declared Patroness of Ponce en Puerto Rico.
1767 – Expelled Jesuits take her image and devotion throughout the world.
1895 – Our Lady of Guadalupe is crowned.
1910 – Pius X declares Our Lady of Guadalupe, Patroness of Latin America.
1911 – A church is built on the site of Juan Bernardino's home.
1921 – Anarchist Luciano Perez places a bomb before the altar on November 14.
1924 – A Codex from the 16th century found by Marshall H. Saville (1867-1935).
1928 – Crowning of the Image in Santa Fe, Argentina.
1929 – Alfonso Marcué detects the image of a bearded man in the right eye.
1935 – Pius XI extends the Patronage of Our Lady of Guadalupe to the Philippines.
1945 – Declared "Queen of Mexico and Empress of the Americas."
1946 – Pius XII declares Our Lady of Guadalupe Patroness of the Americas.
1951 – Carlos Salinas finds the reflection of another person in her eyes.
1961 – Pope John XXIII: Our Lady of Guadalupe is the Mother of the Americas.
    Mother and Teacher of the Faith to all the American peoples.
1962 – Dr. Charles Wahlig finds the reflection of two additional persons.
1966 – Paul VI sends a Golden Rose to the Basilica.
1975 – Dr. Enrique Grave, Ophthalmologist examines the eyes.
1976 – Solemn dedication of the New Basilica of Our Lady of Guadalupe.
1979 – Dr. Philip Callahan takes infrared photos. Declares "image is inexplicable."
1979 – John Paul II calls her "Star of the Evangelization" calling her *Mater Americae*.
1979 – Jose Aste Tönsmann finds additional reflections in the eyes.
1988 – December 12 is declared Feast of Our Lady of Guadalupe in the US.
1990 – Juan Diego beatified in Rome by John Paul II.
1990 – John Paul II second visit to the Basilica.

1992 – Chapel for Our Lady of Guadalupe dedicated in St Peter's Basilica.
1998 – Fr. Xavier Escalada S.J. discovers the Codex 1548.
2002 – July 31, 2002 Juan Diego is canonized by John Paul II.

BIBLIOGRAPHY

1491, by Charles C. Mann, Vintage Books Random House, New York, 2006.

A Handbook on Guadalupe, a collection of essays by various authors published by the Franciscan Friars of the Immaculate, New Bedford, Massachusetts, 1996.

Breve Historia de España by Henry Kamen, p. 9; translation by Marta Hernández Salván, Barcelona, Spain, 2009.

Conflict and Conversion in Sixteenth Century Central Mexico: The Augustinian War on and Beyond the Chichimeca Frontier (European Expansion and Indigenous Response), by Robert H. Jackson. Brill Scholarly Publishing, 2013.

De Viris Illustribus, by St Jerome, Scriptura Press, New York City, 2015.

Descubrimiento de un Busto Humano en los Ojos de la Virgen de Guadalupe, by Carlos Salinas Chávez, De La Mora, Manuel. Editorial Tradición, 2nd Edition 1980.

El mito de la fundación de México Tenochtitlan; Revista de Arqueología Mexicana, Especial 62, and *El cactus en México Catálogo Visual* by Enrique Vela, June 2015.

El Norte de Africa en los Milagros de Guadalupe by Gerardo Rodriguez; from *Estudios de Historia de España;* Volume XII, Tome 2, 2010.

Historia Antigua y de la Conquista de Mexico, by Manuel Orozco y Berra, Publ. by Prensa del Gobierno de Mexico, typography by Gonzalo A. Esteva; Mexico, 1870.

Historia de la Conquista de Mexico, by Francisco López de Gómara, Biblioteca Ayacucho, Caracas, Venezuela, 2007.

Historias y Creencias de los Indios de Mexico, p. 65 Relación del origen de los indios que habitan esta Nueva España según sus historias, by Juan de Tovar. Miraguano Ediciones, 2001.

Il Segreto negli Occhi di Maria. Da Nazareth a Guadalupe, by Flavio Ciucani, Edizione Mediterranee, Roma, 2013.

Juan Diego en los Ojos de la Santísima Virgen de Guadalupe, by Carlos Salinas

Chávez. Ediciones Ruiz, 1st Edition 2008.

La Fractura Historiográfica: Las Investigaciones de Edad Media y Renacimiento Desde el Tercer Milenio; by Javier San José Lera, edited by Francisco Javier Burguillo and Laura Mier. Salamanca, Seminario de Estudios Medievales y Renacentistas, 2008.

La vie quotidienne des Aztèques a la veille de la conquête espagnole by Jacques Soustelle; Hachette Littératures; Paris, 1955.

La Virgen de la Patria: Leyenda, Tradición e Historia de la Guadalupana del Tepeyac by Ramón Sánchez Flores. Puebla, Mexico, 1996. Comité Directivo Estatal.

Las Maravillas de la Virgen de Guadalupe, by Padre Angel Peña, O.A.R.; Libros Católicos, Peru, 2017.

Maravilla Americana y Conjunto de Raras Maravillas, Observadas con la Dirección de las Reglas del Arte de la Pintura en la Prodigiosa Imagen de Nuestra Señora de Guadalupe de Mexico, by Miguel Mateo Maldonado y Cabrera. Imprenta Real del Más Antiguo Colegio de San Ildefonso, 1756.

Miguel Cabrera, Pintor Oaxaqueño del Siglo XVIII, by Javier Castro Mantecón, and Manuel Zárate Aquino. Instituto Nacional de Antropología e Historia, Dirección de Monumentos Coloniales; México, 1958.

Nican Mopohua, by Antonio Valeriano translated by Fr. Mario Rojas Sanchez, Grupo Macehual Guadalupano, Huejutla, Mexico, 1978.

Nican Mopohua by Guillermo Ortiz de Montellano. Mexico City, 1990. Universidad Iberoamericana.

Nican Mopohua: Breve Análisis Literario e Histórico by Jesús Galera Lamadrid; Mexico City, 1991. Editorial Jus.

Nican Mopohua: la Narración Más Antigua de las Apariciones Guadalupanas escrita en Nahuatl y Traducida al Español by Primo Feliciano Velázquez. Obra Nacional de la Buena Prensa, Mexico City.

Our Lady of Guadalupe and the Conquest of Darkness, by Warren H. Carroll, Christendom Press, Front Royal, Virginia, 1983.

Our Lady of Guadalupe and the Miracle of the Roses lecture given by Luis Fernando Castaneda Monter at Saint Francis Chapel, Boston, 2013.

The Ancient Cities of the New World: Being Travels and Explorations in Mexico and Central America From 1857-1882, by Désiré Charnay, Translated by J. Gonino, and Helen S. Conant. Published by The Project Gutenberg, 2014.

The Hummingbird and the Hawk: Conquest and Sovereignty in the Valley of Mexico 1503-1541, by R. C. Padden, Torchbooks Paperback, 1970.

The Legend of Saint Christopher by Margaret Hodges, Eerdman's Books for Young Readers, Grand Rapids, Michigan, 2009.

The likeness of unlike things: insight, enlightenment and the metaphoric way, by David Pimm. Published in *For the Learning of Mathematics* 30, 1; March 2010 FLM Publishing Association, Edmonton, Alberta, Canada.

The Spanish History of Our Lady of Guadalupe Prior to the 16th Century Apparitions in Mexico, by Sister Gabriel, OP, 1900.

The Wonder of Guadalupe, by Francis Johnston, TAN books, Rockford, Illinois, 1981.

Tonantzin Guadalupe: Pensamiento Náhuatl y Mensaje Cristiano en el Nican Mopohua by Miguel León Portilla. Mexico City, 2000. El Colegio Nacional, Fondo de Cultura Económica.

ABOUT THE AUTHOR

Carlos Caso-Rosendi, is an Argentine-American writer. He was born in 1954 in Esquel, a small town in the western Patagonia region of Argentina. His parents, fallen away Catholics, involved the family with a pseudo-Christian cult when Carlos was thirteen years old. That very year he entered a prestigious technical school in Buenos Aires. There he studied English, Math, Physics, and various other technical disciplines. Later on his parents discontinued his schooling on the advise of the sectarian leaders who discouraged superior education for their youths. On reaching the age of majority Carlos left the sect and eventually immigrated to the United States where he completed his technical studies.

Having lost interest in religious matters, he continued steadily to read Classics on his own, seeking to somehow complete his interrupted education. In 1996 he had a completely unexpected personal insight that convinced him of the existence of God. A friend recommended him to read C. S. Lewis and later, guided by Lewis and other contemporary Christian writers, he set to read all the classic works of Christianity. In doing so he convinced himself that the Catholic Church was the original Church founded by Jesus Christ having Christ's authority to teach the truth about God's purpose and man's destiny.

He was received in the Catholic Church on Assumption Day 2001, at the Cathedral of the Most Precious Blood of Christ, London, England under the auspices of Cardinal Cormac Murphy-O'Connor, receiving Baptism, Confirmation and First Communion on that day. He is the author of *Ark of Grace – Our Blessed Mother in Holy Scripture, A Vademecum of Catholic Apologetics, Guadalupe: A River of Light,* and *They Asked for a Sign..*

OFFERING

This book is offered in reparation for offenses and blasphemies against the Blessed Virgin Mary.

Hail Mary, full of grace.
The Lord is with thee.
Blessed art thou amongst women,
and blessed is the fruit of thy womb, Jesus.
Holy Mary, Mother of God,
pray for us sinners,
now and at the hour of our death.
Amen.

Made in the USA
Monee, IL
18 February 2023

28177731R00083